Taxes for Small Business

The Ultimate Guide to Small Business Taxes Including LLC Taxes, Payroll Taxes, and Self-Employed Taxes as a Sole Proprietorship

Contents

Introduction

Filing taxes is something every business in America needs to do and there is a lot that needs to be learned in this process. To get the most out of your tax return for you and your business, it should be a job that is looked at several times a year.

It does not matter if you are self-employed or a limited liability company (LLC). You need to know what the difference is regarding taxes and how to get the most out of your return.

Payroll taxes may seem scary. However, you will start to see how simple they are as you read through Chapter 2. Do you know what deductions you can make as an individual taxpayer and as a business? There are so many tax breaks for a small business that you need to consider. On December 2017, President Trump signed and passed the Tax Cuts and Jobs Act. You will see the updated information for deductions and credits that are available to you based on the new GOP tax bill. Best of all, learn how to make the new tax bill work for you so you can maximize your deductions.

With the help of this book, you will learn how you can get through those grueling audits and survive the pressure of Uncle Sam and his squad of tax informants. If you have not filed the previous year's taxes, then you may want to check out Chapter 5 as we discuss IRS survival and this particular issue.

If you take anything away from this book, I want you to focus on one chapter. Read Chapter 6 and learn how to make your business taxes work for your business. Once you have read that chapter, I know you will want to continue reading. I encourage you to start from the beginning and learn how everything in this book will bring you full circle and help you file your taxes. The aim of this book is to show you what you need to do so your business not only survives but also thrives.

As a special bonus, check out Chapter 7 to get examples of each of the IRS forms discussed throughout the chapters so you can see what they look like and their purpose.

Chapter 1 – Differences Between LLC and Self-Employed Taxes

All small businesses have one thing in common. They need to file taxes. It does not matter if you are self-employed or have a limited liability company (LLC), the IRS will still expect you to file your taxes every year.

Self-Employed or Sole Proprietorship Taxes

When you are self-employed or unaffiliated, you are taxed strictly on your own income. Therefore, when you file taxes you are simply calculating your total income and subtracting your total expenses or damages. This makes it easy to figure out your net income.

Being a Sole Proprietor, you are responsible or liable for everything that happens in your business. Sole proprietorship can be businesses such as freelancing, home-based or a retail trade business. As you are the only person involved, all expenses, debts and income are yours only. That means that anything that happens with your business will be on your shoulders. You are the boss and there is no one above you.

As all income and expenses pass through you as the owner, you need to declare those on your personal tax return. Make sure that when filing your taxes, you are filing or registering the business portion on a Schedule C or C-EZ and include it with your Form 1040.

If you work for a company as an employee or clerk you receive a W-2. This W-2 is a record of all your earnings and the employer has already subtracted your taxes from your paycheck. However, when you go into business for yourself things get a bit trickier. It does not matter if you own a bakery, drive for Uber, or have a consulting firm, you are your own boss and you must file your taxes.

Limited Liability Company (LLC) Taxes

Through an LLC you can be taxed as either a sole proprietorship, a partnership or a corporation. This is based on the number of members. The owner of the LLC is taxed individually only on their share of the company. When the LLC is set up you will determine the size of each member's responsibility and as elected, you will be responsible for any losses or gains of the company.

If you are planning to form an LLC, you should know that the IRS recognizes a single-owner as a sole proprietorship when filing taxes. Therefore, you would file your taxes on a Schedule C for a sole-owner LLC.

Through a multi-owner LLC, taxes start to become different when filing. Each owner will receive their portion of the business profits. These will be filed on a Schedule E and be attached to your individual tax return. As you have an LLC formed, you will need to file a form 1065 with the IRS. This form is also used by a partnership. It is to ensure you are reporting the correct amount of income. As an LLC you will need to provide a Schedule K-1 to each of the members. The Schedule K-1 is a breakdown of the profits and losses for each member share in the LLC.

Differences

One of the major differences between being self-employed and forming an LLC is that when you are self-employed you are responsible for all gains and losses of the company, whereas, if you form an LLC, you are only required to report the portion of the company you are responsible for. This gives you extra protection and assurance, especially if you have partners.

The benefits of being self-employed are that you do not need to worry about complex tax forms and you will report the taxes on a Schedule C when filing your personal taxes. When running a single-owner LLC you enjoy the same benefits as a self-employed. However, with a multi-owner LLC or a partnership LLC the company return is done on behalf of the owner. That means the owners pay taxes based on their partnership income or the income they receive through the partnership.

It is a great idea if you are considering being self-employed to discuss your options and preferences with your attorney, accountant or advisor. The advice you'll get on how to form the different entities will most likely vary depending on where you live. Every state has different requirements for filing and paying taxes.

Chapter 2 – Payroll Taxes and How to Best Manage Them

Any business who has employees will need to understand payroll taxes. Most business owners hire this out because it is not the most enjoyable part of the business. However, if you have only a handful employees, you can save time and money by doing it yourself. To do this, you need to get some knowledge regarding the payroll and the taxes that come with it. This chapter is aimed at introducing you to payroll taxes so you can get a better understanding of the processes involved. Once you understand payroll, it will no longer feel like a scary event to avoid.

Preparation

One thing that is key to your payroll success is preparation. Before you ever hire employees, you will need to plan and prepare the payroll. That is, you need to do the calculations, estimation, forecast, processing, and decide who will do the payroll for the business.

First, we need to know what taxes are withheld from your employee's paycheck and what your responsibilities are with the payroll tax. Here is the list of taxes that are withheld from the paycheck:

- ➤ Withholding of Federal, State and Local income taxes

- ➤ Withholding of FICA and paying an equal amount as an employer

- ➤ Based on the employee's pay, you will need to pay unemployment taxes

- ➤ Based on the employee's pay, you will need to pay the State and Federal worker's compensation funds

These taxes are a given for each employee. However, as an employer you also have specific responsibilities related to the payroll taxes. These responsibilities will help you to comply with the laws.

- ➤ **Withhold or take out the appropriate taxes**
  - ○ These taxes will include: Federal, State and Local income taxes based on the employee's election on the W4.
  - ○ FICA taxes for both the employee and employer based off a percentage of the gross pay.

- ➤ **Set aside funds**
  - ○ Includes the employers' and employees' Social Security and Medicare
  - ○ Employers' liabilities for unemployment taxes and workers compensation.

- ➤ **Pay the taxes**
  - ○ Make sure you pay your taxes to the right agencies.
    - ▪ Example: Federal income taxes and Social Security/Medicare will be paid to the IRS.
  - ○ This will include employee and employer taxes.

- ➤ **Report tax liabilities**
  - ○ Report your tax liabilities to the right agencies and to the employees based off the specifications of the law.
    - ▪ Form 941 – Employer's Quarterly Wage and Tax Report
    - ▪ Form 940 – Unemployment Tax Report

- ➤ **Provide additional reports**

o Some Federal, State and Local agencies may require additional reports such as reporting the employment status of all new employees.

Be sure you pay the appropriate taxes for all your employees and your business. If you do not pay the taxes, you could acquire some hefty fines and penalties from the IRS. IRS tells us that "employers who do not comply with the employment tax law may be subject to criminal and civil sanctions for willfully or recklessly failing to pay employment (payroll) taxes." However, do not let this alarm you. Here are some steps to take to avoid fines and penalties by the IRS.

I want to make it as easy as possible for you as the employer to prepare for this grueling task of payroll. Before you get started, look at this 12-step checklist. It will help you prepare for your employees and ensure you are on the right track.

1. Get an Employer ID Number

If you have employees or plan to have employees, you will need an Employer ID Number. This number is a unique EIN that will identify your business to the Federal government. It is much like a Social Security Number for your business.

It is not hard to get an EIN. In fact, it is rather easy. You can get one online through the IRS website, by phone or fax in the form. You do not need an attorney to fill out the form. However, if you have questions pertaining to the form you can consult one and they will be able to help and advice you.

2. Register as an Employer with Your State

Through the state's department of revenue, you will need to register as an employer. Keep in mind, if your state has income taxes you need each employee to fill out a form W-4. As each state is different you will need to find out what the state's requirements are such as what taxes need to be withheld and the time table you need to follow when reporting those withholdings. Some state's may have unemployment and worker's compensation as well as additional items that need to be deducted. Check or research with your state to get a complete list of items.

3. Register with the IRS for Payroll Taxes

For an employer to register for payroll taxes you need to go online to the IRS website and register through the Electronic Federal Tax Payment System (EFTPS). This is so you can make payroll tax deposits and file payroll tax reports. All you need to do is provide and add information about your business and the bank account information and data where the payments and cash are coming from.

4. Sign Up for the State New Hire Registration System

When you have employees, you must register them with their state. All the states share and contribute a common system for this registration. The goal of this system is for tracking or to be able to go after employees who owe money for child support and other debts. In that way their pay can be garnished if needed. You can always sign up to use the system now even though you're the only one in your business. Then as you get new employees you will be able to use the system for them right away.

5. Get Ready to Verify Employment Eligibility

When you hire a new employee, they must provide proof, information and verification of their eligibility or qualification to work in the United States. There are two methods you could use to accomplish this. To manifest verification, you need to fill out the standard I-9 form. If your state requires it, you will need to enroll in the E-verify system. Either way you will still need your new employees to fill out a I-9. From there you can either go from the form or use the E-verify system.

6. Sign Up for Worker's Compensation Insurance

Make sure you have worker's compensation insurance. This is paid by your business to provide the benefits to your employees who become ill, down or injured on the job. It can be purchased either through a commercial carrier, self-insured basis or your state's program for Worker's Compensation Insurance.

7. Sign Up for Unemployment Insurance

Sometimes you may need to terminate an employee. It is important that your business has unemployment insurance as this is paid by the company. The Federal unemployment insurance tax must be paid by the employer. Also, there are some states who may require an unemployment insurance tax to be paid as well. Do your research for your state so you know what to expect.

8. Get Required Workplace Posters

If you have employees, then you are required to have specific posters posted for them to read and understand their rights and claim. You can get more information and instruction on this through the Department of Labor.

9. Gather New Hire Paperwork and Forms

Before your employees can start receiving their paycheck you will need to collect and gather some paperwork from them. Consider this your new hire packet. You will need to keep this packet on file for all your employees. At the minimum, you will need the following in this packet.

1. **Form W-4 for Federal Income Tax Withholding**

    a. You will need to keep this on file while your employee is employed at the business.

    b. Your employee can change this at any time. Always keep the most current on file.

2. **Form I-9 and E-Verify System for Employment Eligibility**

a. You will need to keep this on file and attached with any documents that are provided by the E-Verify System.

3. **Job Application Form**

   a. Every applicant must fill out a job application. Keep this and their resume on file with their employment packet.

   b. If you need to do a background check it will also be included with this application.

   c. You will also have a statement included that states that the applicant is testifying that everything is true and is signed by them.

4. **State Withholding and Registration**

   a. Every employer must register their new hires into the state's new hire notification system. Keep a record of the confirmation in your employee's file. This will ensure you have inputted them into the system in case you are audited.

5. **A Checklist of New Hire Training and Tasks**

   a. Many times you may have a task that needs to be completed by a specific date. Give your new hire a checklist of this that also contains a section where they can write the date when it was completed. Once completed, they need to sign, and date then include it in the employees file.

6. **Your Employee Handbook**

   a. Ensure that all new hires have received the employee handbook.

   b. Have them sign a form that states that they have read and understood what is in the handbook. You may want to go over the areas you most want them to understand and have them repeat each area. As you update the handbook, have them sign a new form and keep the most current in their file.

10. Set Up Your Payroll System

You will be responsible of ensuring there is an excellent record and payroll system in place. This includes payroll taxes such as withholding taxes and periodic reports and payments.

11. Create and Use an Employee Handbook (As mentioned in 9.6)

There is no law that states you need an employee handbook. However, it is a smart thing to have. This handbook will outline your policies, duties, mission, business statement, etc. Anything you need the employee to know about the company and job should be listed in this handbook. When the new employee receives the handbook, you should have them sign a statement that they received it.

12. Know the Employment and Labor Laws

It is always wise to know the employment and labor laws (both federal and state). Do your research and investigation. Even though you have an employee handbook, you should have a company handbook that covers everything in the handbooks for the employees and include anything extra that you need to know when running your business.

Time to Pay Your Employees and Deduct Taxes

You are all set. Now you need to hire your employees and start getting them into the system, so they will get paid. Although, where do we start? Before you can pay your employee, you will need to calculate and determine the taxes that should come out of their pay. The first thing you need to obtain from your employee is a current W-4 form. This should be included in your employees' folder and updated and amended at minimum yearly. As an employer, do not offer advice on what to put down on this form. However, you can provide simple instruction, which is also included in the form. For your convenience, I have included some brief instructions, so you can ensure the form is filed out correctly when receiving it from your employee.

Let's say your employee and his wife both work. They also have three children who live with them at home.

> On line A, your employee will enter 1 to claim himself. Because his spouse works, your employee will put a 0 on line B.

> On line C, they will inter the number of dependent children they have. In the example, they would enter 3 on line C.

> Then on line H, they will add up the numbers and enter this into the form W-4.

Once the employee turns in their form W-4, you will need to start calculating the taxes. Be sure to apply and implement the IRS rules for computing and enumerating the federal tax withholdings from the gross pay of each employee. To help with this, I have included a basic outline to help you with this task.

> Start by determining the gross pay for your employee. That means you verify hourly wages, tips and bonus compensation. This includes anything that the employee has earned before any deductions.

> From the W-4 form your employee submitted, locate their filing status. This will either be single, married, etc. Highlight this information so it will be easy to find each time you are figuring out the payroll taxes.

> Locate the number of allowances that were inputted. This information will also be on the W-4 form. It is how many people the employee is claiming or declaring. Refer to the IRS tax handouts for the accurate and detailed charts to determine the correct amount to be deducted based on the number of

exemptions. It can be wise to highlight the number of exemptions and write the amount on a sticky note that can be put on the form. Be sure to verify this amount each time you do the payroll just in case the IRS has updated or changed their policies. This is especially crucial around the first of each year.

Now that we have the information we need from the W-4 form, it is time to go to the IRS tax calculator. The withholdings calculator will request specific information. Input this information to ensure you have an accurate withholding amount. It will ask for the worker's tax filing status and the number of dependents they are claiming. The app will also require you to enter the gross wages and how often they get paid such as weekly, bi-weekly, monthly, etc.

➢ Through the app you will need to input the total year-to-date federal withholdings. The system will take this information and withdraw it from the required amount owed for the year.

➢ Once you have used the app to determine the wages to be held you need to refer to the IRS publication 15 to determine how much you should be withholding. Once you figure out how much is subject to withholdings, refer to the official IRS tables to determine how much you should withhold. You will need to make sure you are looking at the right section based on the W-4 form and the pay period.

Make sure you keep a good report on a spreadsheet to help you keep all this information organized. In that way, when you create the pay statement you have all the information at your fingertips. On the spreadsheet include a column for all deductions you need to take out of your employees pay.

The next one we need to calculate is the Social Security withholdings. This is a federal program providing retirement and disability income. It is funded through tax withholdings.

- In 2018, the Social Security withholding is 6.2% of the gross pay for each employee. Keep in mind, this is subject to change throughout the year or yearly. Therefore, keep checking to ensure you have the most up-to-date percentage.

- An employee must continue to pay this tax until they reach the base limit. If the employee hits this limit, then they are not subject to paying the tax.

- For 2018 that base limit is $128,400.

- If you are self-employed or run a company owned by one individual, you will pay a higher Social Security tax rate. This rate is currently 15.3% for 2018

Your employees will also have Medicare withholdings. This goes to toward Medicare to help provide medical coverage for both elderly and disabled. It is funded through the payroll tax withholdings.

- In 2018, the Medicare tax rate is set at 1.45% for both the employer and the employee. However, if you are self-employed the rate is 3.3%. There is no base limit to the Medicare tax. This means that your dollars are subject to withholdings.

Now that you have the basic and main withholdings, we need to look at other withholdings your business may have. This will include any benefits the business offers to your employees' as an option but is not mandatory. Some of these may be deducted before taxes are taken out, such as a retirement plan. In this case it will reduce the amount of pay that is subject tax.

- The most common type of retirement plan that is offered by most businesses is a 401(k). Contributions to this plan is based off a pre-tax. The company may also offer a matching contribution to these plans.

> A health spending arrangement (FSA) is another type of benefit that may be offered by the company. This is a voluntary arrangement between the employee and employer to help with medical expense reimbursement.

> You may also give an option for a health savings account (HSA) which is like the FSA. However, the money in this account does not roll over at the end of the year.

As with any business who has employees, you need to calculate the State and Federal Unemployment taxes. Remember, unemployment tax is paid by the employers. Although, the system will combine the federal unemployment tax system with your state program.

> Always pay your state unemployment tax first. This way when the company files taxes it can take a credit on the federal unemployment tax that has already been paid.

When you have employees, you will find that not all employee taxes are alike. That means you will need to find the state guidelines for all your employees. When you have employees from many different states, you will need to find the proper tax rates for each one based on that state. A good example would be the military. Each soldier will be taxed based on their home of record and not the base or location they are found in.

> A tip is to start by researching the individual's state Department of Revenue or the taxation for the state.

> You already know how to calculate the taxes for federal. Once you have the tax rates for each state, you can calculate the rates the same way as you did for the federal taxes.

Make sure you report your tax withholdings on the proper forms. Remember that for each type of payroll tax, a different tax form will be needed. A great way to stay on top of this is considering a payroll company. There are other options if you cannot outsource your payroll.

➢ There is some great account software available. This software will help you with all your calculations. However, if you do use software make sure you are always up-to-date. Due to tax laws changing, your payroll software will need to change, although we have this great thing called the internet. You could try a cloud-based version of the software and it will allow you to access it from anywhere and it will always be up-to-date.

➢ Most of the tax authorities will allow you to pay your taxes electronically. This is great, especially if you use a cloud-based software.

➢ Although, if you do decide to choose a payroll company, they will take your employee data and input it for you. The great thing about this is that the payroll company is required to always have their software up-to-date and they keep the tax codes updated too.

Payroll Tax in a Nut Shell

Every employee you hire will have payroll taxes deducted. As their employer, this is your responsibility, although withholding those taxes is not the end. What do you do with all that tax money? You will need to make deposits of your payroll taxes either semi-weekly or monthly. This will be based on the size of your company. The areas to look at for these taxes are the following.

➢ Consider the amount you withheld from your employees that pay for federal and state income taxes.

➢ Don't forget about the deductions you took for Social Security and Medicare.

➢ As an employer you will also need to pay your Social Security and Medicare.

- ➢ You will need to ensure you are making payments and filing the federal unemployment tax regularly.

- ➢ Don't forget to make payroll tax deposits to all the states involved (if your employees are from different states).

- ➢ You can make these deposits on a form 8109. However, everything is now electronic. I would advise using the form 8109 to keep for your records and then transfer the information to the IRS Electronic Filing System (EFTPS). This will simplify things and you will not find yourself hunting for the information as you are making the deposits.

All businesses who have employees and need to pay the payroll taxes are required to report those taxes regularly. This means you must do the following.

- ➢ Make sure you report your payroll tax liabilities on Form 941. This needs to be done quarterly.

- ➢ You will also need to report the annual unemployment tax on a Form 944.

- ➢ Do not forget to report the state unemployment and worker's compensation.

When you are working with your payroll, it is a great idea to create and maintain a payroll register. If you use an online accounting system this feature is already available. However, a good old excel spreadsheet works as well. Keep it organized as it does get filled with your payroll tax reports at the end of the year. In this registry you should include the following.

- ➢ The total gross wages for all employees. Include the total social security wages (only up to the maximum for each employee) and the total medical wages.

- ➢ The total federal, state and local taxes held from each employee's pay.

> Any optional donations that were held from the employee's pay. This is to include charitable giving, union dues and anything else that may have been elected.

> You will also need to set aside what is equal to the social security and Medicare deductions.

Once you have all this done you will need to set up a Yearly Tax Calendar. This is very important and needs to be created and maintained. That means, do not create it and just leave it. Take the extra time to maintain the calendar. You will find that it makes it easier to track all the payroll taxes for each employee. If you use an accounting software, you can use that to keep a calendar or you can do it manually. Either way works. Make sure you add your states in the calendar with the federal. I want you to remember that the reports you need to generate for payroll taxes are for federal income taxes, FICA taxes (Social Security and Medicare taxes) and federal unemployment taxes. Sometimes you will hear federal and FICA taxes called the 941 taxes. This is due to being reported on form 941. Keep in mind that there are some states that do not have income taxes. However, if you have states that do, you will also need to include those and report them to the states involved.

There is one thing to think about: if you do not have employees and instead hire an independent contractor you are not required to withhold income and FICA taxes from their pay. The contractor will worry about this. However, you are required to complete an annual report for the contractor and send it to the IRS.

Before you make your calendar, determine if you need to make your payroll tax deposits on a semi-weekly, monthly or a quarterly basis.

> **Semi-Weekly:** If you have a large business with many employees you may need to make your payroll deposits twice a week. If your payroll taxes are more than $50,000, you will need to make deposits on the semi-weekly schedule. If you

have payroll paid on a Saturday, Sunday, Monday or Tuesday the deposit will be made on the following Friday. If you have payroll paid on a Wednesday, Thursday or Friday the deposits are due on the following Wednesday. Keep in mind, if your payroll is $100,000 or more you need to make daily deposits for the current year and the next year.

> **Monthly:** If you have payroll taxes less than $50,000 you can make deposits monthly. Tax payments will be due on the last day of the month or by the 15th of each month. Keep in mind, if the due date is during a weekend or holiday the taxes will be due the next business day.

> **Quarterly:** Remember, these are deposited with a form 941 and are due by the end of the month following the end of the quarter. Which means, your quarterly payroll taxes are due by the end of the first month of the new quarter. Although, if you have made all your payroll taxes on time and in full throughout the months, you will have until the 10th of the first month into the new quarter to file your 941 form.

> **Federal unemployment tax:** If your business liabilities are over $500, the deposit for unemployment is due by the end of the first month going into the new quarter.

> **Yearly:** Every year you will need to provide a W-2 form for each of your employees' and a 1099-MISC form for any contractor that you have. This are due by the last day in January. The federal unemployment tax report and any deposits are due by the end of January for the previous year with the use of a 940 form. If all deposits are in full and on time, the form is due by the 10th of the next month. For your employees' you will need to transmit or file a W-3 form with the W-2 form. This is for the transmittal to Social Security. For your contractors you will use a 1096 form to go along with any of the 1099s forms. These are also due by the end of January.

I want you to keep in mind, this schedule is for federal taxes only. Each state has their own schedule and you would need to check with those states to get the most up-to-date and accurate schedule for your state.

State and Federal Income Taxes

We have been taking a lot about taxes and mainly payroll taxes. You may have noticed that I have mentioned State and Federal taxes. From both an individual and business point of view, it is essential that you know the difference between the two. Otherwise, you may end up owing money to both the State and Federal Government. Make sure you do not get the two taxes mixed up or think they are the same.

Federal Income Tax: It does not matter what state you live in; you are always subject to Federal Income Tax. This is the same for both individuals and businesses. If you reside and work within the 50 states, you will pay Uncle Sam. The amount of taxes you pay each year is based on your yearly income level. Within the United States, we have a progressive tax system. What that means is that the more income you make, the more federal taxes you will pay.

December 2017, President Trump passed a bill for a new tax law. Within this tax law, the seven tax brackets changed. This new bill took effect January 2018. Below is the new tax bracket.

SINGLE			
NEW RATE	**NEW INCOME BRACKET**	**OLD RATE**	**OLD INCOME BRACKET**
10%	Up to $9,525	10%	Up to $9,525
12%	$9,525 to $38,700	15%	$9,525 to $38,700
22%	38,700 to $82,500	25%	$38,700 to 93,700
24%	$82,500 to $157,500	28%	$93,700 to $195,450
32%	$157,500 to $200,000	33%	$195,450 to $424,950
35%	$200,000 to $500,000	35%	$424,950 to $426,700
37%	$500,000+	39.60%	$426,700+

MARRIED, FILED JOINTLY			
NEW RATE	**NEW INCOME BRACKET**	**OLD RATE**	**OLD INCOME BRACKET**
10%	Up to $19,050	10%	Up to $19,050
12%	$19,050 to $77,400	15%	$19,050 to $77,400
22%	$77,400 to $165,000	25%	$77,400 to $156,150
24%	$165,000 to $315,000	28%	$156,150 to $237,950
32%	$315,000 to $400,000	33%	$237,950 to $424,950
35%	$400,000 to $600,000	35%	$424,950 to $480,050
37%	$600,000+	39.60%	$480,050+

As the tax changes are made it is important to stay informed of the new laws. Most people have taxes deducted from their paycheck in a pay-as-you-go tax system. Then this is sent to the IRS for them. However, if you own a business, you are the one who is sending these taxes to IRS for your employees. For independent contractors, freelancers, etc., these taxes are handled by the individuals and they are responsible for sending the information to the IRS and to pay taxes throughout the year,

If you do not pay enough throughout the year, then when you file taxes at year's end, you will have to pay the remaining amount. Although, the opposite is also true, if you paid too much in taxes you will be getting that money back. Such a day can be a nice payday.

State Income Taxes: These taxes are different from the Federal tax laws that are enforced by the IRS. Keep in mind, these taxes are governed by the individual states tax commission. Therefore, it is on a state-by-state basis. They can vary depending on your job, state, etc. Here's one thing that is the same with the Federal tax laws: the state laws are also on a progressive tax system.

Although, even though most states are taxed based on their income, it is still regulated by the individual state. For example, in Pennsylvania they have a flat tax. That means, regardless of how much you make the tax rate will be the same for everyone. There are other states that do not have a state tax at all. States like Wyoming, Washington, Texas, South Dakota, Florida and Alaska are the seven states that do not have a state income tax imposed. Along with this, you also have Tennessee and New Hampshire that only have a state tax imposed on income that is from dividends and interest.

With both state and federal taxes, you have until 15 April of the following year to file. Keep in mind that each state may be different, and you will want to check with your state to ensure you are filing on time. The filing date is also the same for businesses.

Alternative Minimum Tax (AMT)

Now that we've been talking about state and federal income taxes, we also need to discuss the Alternative Minimum Tax (AMT). Most of us do not know anything about this tax. It is a supplemental income tax that is imposed by the United States Federal Government. However, there is an additional baseline on income tax for individuals, corporations, estates and trusts who have exemptions or even special circumstances that will allow for a lower payment of the standard income tax.

The real question is who must pay this tax? When a taxpayer is making a certain income, it will trigger the AMT. When you are in a higher tax bracket and qualify for the AMT, it will eliminate many of the deductions to ensure you pay some tax.

Although, because of the new bill that was put into effect by President Trump, instead of 5 million being affected by the AMT in 2017, now only 200,000 tax payers are affected.

Many taxpayers do not know about AMT and those who do may not know how it works. It is different from regular tax rates. With AMT you do not have standard deductions or personal exemptions. Although, if you do not have standard deductions, that means you also do not have itemized deductions. However, it does include other streams of income that is not normally counted in regular income taxes such as exercising incentive stock options. Keep in mind that AMT tax rates are like the regular tax rates. Based off the new bill:

STATUS	2018 - 2025	
	EXEMPTION	PHASEOUT
Single/Head of Household	$70,300	$500,000
Married Filing Jointly	$109,400	$1M
Married Filing Seperately	N/A	N/A

I am sure you are wondering if you fall into this tax. Think of it this way, if your adjusted gross income is above the exemptions then you will need to calculate AMT. That means you may need to calculate AMT and pay the higher rate. This is done in a 6251 form. Keep this in mind that once you qualify for the AMT, you must pay it. Although, you can work on lowering it for next year.

You will find that AMT tax will mainly target married taxpayers. This is because they usually have a higher income and could fall into these brackets. Also, AMT does not have any marriage bonus.

Chapter 3 – Knowing Your Tax Deductions, Exemptions and Credits

It does not matter if you are doing your individual taxes or your business taxes. You need to know and understand your tax deductions, exemptions and credits. The main difference between them is that deductions and exemptions will reduce your taxable income. Whereas, your credits will reduce your tax.

Any deductions and exceptions will reduce taxes within your tax bracket. However, any credits will reduce the dollars regardless of the tax bracket.

The Differences

Exemptions

Exemptions only concern themselves with people and the relationship you have with them. Other than determining if someone is or is not your dependent, there is no financial basis. Keep in mind, the higher your exemptions, the more reduction of your taxable income. Basically, you are telling IRS that you have this many people in the home living off your income. This will put more income into your pocket each month and less taxes will be taken out. If you have any questions about who you can claim as a dependent, you can refer to the IRS publication 501.

Deductions

Deductions are directly related to the expenses you incurred through the course of the tax year. While deductions are related to expenses, they are impacted and varies according to two criteria. They can be scaled based on above-the-line or below-the-line expenses. Another distinction gets added if they are itemized or standard deductions.

Above-the-line: These deductions are used in the configuration of figuring your AGI. This is before you decide if you are going to itemize your deductions or take the standard deduction. Which means, these deductions are yours to take regardless if you itemize or not.

Below-the-line: These deductions are itemized. However, some can only be taken if the expenses will exceed a specific percentage of your AGI. That means, these deductions can double your deductions and be very useful.

Itemized Deductions: These deductions are a list that are recorded on a schedule A. It would be beneficial to itemize your deductions and compare them with the standard deductions. By doing this you will see which type of deduction will give you the bigger return. Here are a few things to think about if you are to itemize your deductions.

> ➢ Have itemized deductions totaled more than the standard deduction?

> ➢ Did you have a large amount of uninsured medical and dental expenses?

> ➢ Did you pay mortgage interest and real estate taxes for your home?

> ➢ Did you have a large amount of unreimbursed expenses as an employee?

> ➢ Did you have a large amount of uninsured casualty (fire, flood, wind, etc.) or theft losses?

> ➢ Did you make any large contributions to a qualified charity?

> ➢ Did you have any large amount of unreimbursed miscellaneous expenses?

If your itemized deductions are less than the standard amount you may still want to consider itemizing your deductions.

Standard Deductions: Based on your filing status and age, the IRS allows you to deduct a fixed dollar amount from your taxable income. There is a standard cut off with a standard deduction. This usually increases each year due to inflation. A standard deduction is a good way to make your taxes easier to file. However, it does not mean it is always the best choice. You should do the calculations and find out what would be the most cost effective for you.

To learn more about the deductions you may want to refer to the IRS publication 505: Tax Withholding and Estimated Tax.

Credits

When you receive credits, they are incentives that are generally aimed at influencing the behavior. Credits can be many things. Think of it as a reward in some ways. You can get credits back when you file taxes for things such as education credit, residential energy credit, child tax credit and adoption credit. These credits will have separate lines on your 1040 form.

You will find that there are a lot of tax credits for a small business. Here is a list of just a few. However, do your research and you will find so many more that can be added to this list.

Car and Truck Expenses: Most businesses have a car or truck that is used in the business. If you are required to record and prove the use of the vehicle for the business, then you can deduct the cost of operating and maintaining the vehicle. Keep an accurate record of the mileage, gasoline and oil changes.

Salaries and Wages: Keep in mind, if you are a sole proprietor, partner or an LLC member and take out draws from the business, these are nondeductible. However, if you have employees you can deduct their payments.

Contract Labor: There are many businesses who use independent contractors to meet their needs. The cost of contracted labor is deductible. Be sure to issue the contractor a 1099-MISC form.

Rent on Business Property: If you rent space such as an office, storefront, factory or any other type of facility then it is fully deductible.

Depreciation: Depreciation is allowed when you purchase a property for your small business. This also includes Section 179 for the purchase of equipment up to $500,000. It could also receive a 50% bonus depreciation.

Supplies: Every business needs supplies. For example, if you are a cleaning service and need cleaning supplies, then they are fully deductible.

Utilities: For your facility, your electricity is fully deductible. You can also include business cell phone charges. If you have a home office deduction, the cost of your first landline is not deductible but if you have a second line it can be deducted.

Repairs: You can fully deduct the cost of ordinary repairs and maintenance. Even though there are some exceptions, if the repairs and maintenance add to the value of the property, it must be capitalized and recovered through depreciation.

Insurance: All businesses need some sort of insurance. Your business owner's policy, malpractice coverage and business continuation insurance are fully deductible. Health coverage can be deducted. Many qualify to claim this type of credit up to 50% of the premiums.

Commissions: Any commissions are fully deductible.

Advertising: Advertising cost are fully deductible. Like with everything else with your business, keep all your receipts. If you are advertising in your local paper they will give you a receipt for your bookkeeping.

Travel: If you or a staff member needs to travel out of town for your business, the cost of transportation and lodging are fully deductible. Be sure to keep your receipt for all business expenses related to the travel. For all the requirements for business trips refer to the IRS publication 463. Be sure to claim any travel expenses on the schedule C.

Conventions: This is one deduction that is always overlooked. Many businesses have conventions you can attend. If the convention is directly related to your business, you can claim the business expenses. Keep in mind, you can only claim two conventions per year. Some conventions include meals in the price. If this is the case, you cannot deduct your meals or any items that is covered by the cost of the convention. However, if the cost does not include your meals or entertainment, you may be able to deduct up to 50% of the cost.

Home Office: For a home office we hit a grey area. The home needs to be used regularly and exclusively as the principle place of business. You can claim deductions for the painting of the office space, which is a direct cost. As an indirect cost you can deduct a percentage of rent or mortgage interest and real estate taxes, which will reflect the percentage of the business use of the home. These are not the only deductions you can claim for your home office. If you have a home office, do your research and make sure you claim everything you can pertaining to your home office.

Legal and Professional Fees: Fees for legal and accounting are fully deductible. Which means, any time you see your accountant or need legal advice and you are billed, it is deductible for your business. This also includes consulting fees.

Meals and Entertainment: You can deduct up to 50% of business meals. You can only claim this if it is a substantiate expense. You can refer to the IRS 463 form.

Rent on Machinery and Equipment: Fees that are paid to lease or rent items or equipment for business use are fully deductible.

Interest on Business Indebtedness: Any interest on loans the business takes out are fully deductible.

Employee Benefit Programs and Qualified Retirement Plans: The cost of these employee benefit plans is deductible.

Mortgage Interest: If your business owns realty, the mortgage interest can be fully deducted.

There are so many ways to make the IRS work for you to save money. Many times, we forget some of the most important deductions and credits. Although, how do you qualify for these great money-saving opportunities? In fact, these are so over looked that even the IRS wants to ensure you are claiming all the credits you can. Here are a few that I want you to be able to qualify for. They are the top eight that give you the greatest deduction and credit.

Charitable Donations (also includes travel expenses): Keep in mind we talked about itemizing your deductions. For those who do itemize their deductions, you know that charitable donations are deductible. This includes both cash and goods contributions. One thing most people do not realize or forget is any travel you do for a charity is also deductible. For example, let's say you have seen the soup kitchens. You can deduct either your actual expenses or the standard rate of 14 cents per mile. The IRS also says you can claim the following for travel:

- ➢ Air, Rail and Bus fares
- ➢ Out-of-pocket expenses for a car
- ➢ Taxi fares
- ➢ Meals

Keep in mind that the IRS does say you cannot mix charity and vacation and expect to get a deduction. This means no sightseeing if you are on a trip for charity. For more information on this you can checkout page 5 of the IRS publication 526 on Charitable Contributions.

State Sales Tax: This is one of the best kept secrets. Many people are not aware that you can deduct your state and local income taxes or your state and local sales tax. For those who are lucky enough to live in a non-income tax state, this one is easy, and you can deduct your sales tax without problems. For the rest of us you can choose between the type of tax you deduct. Be sure to deduct the one that will give you the biggest deduction.

Child and Dependent Care Credit: If you have children or dependents you may overlook this one. It is most commonly associated with children under 12 as your dependent. If you need to put them into child care when you work or when looking for a job, then you can deduct those expenses. If you are looking after someone who is elderly or disabled and you need to hire someone to watch them while you work, you can also deduct that cost.

Retirement Savings Contributions Credit: Also known as the Saver's Credit. If you are a low-income individual who is putting away for retirement you may qualify for this deduction. Here are specific requirements that must be met.

➤ Older than 18

➤ Cannot be claimed as a dependent by someone else

➤ Not attending school full-time

➤ Meets the income eligibility

Earned Income Tax Credit: This is one of those controversial credits. Some who never pay into the system may still receive it. Therefore, others are not a fan of it. However, it is also overlooked by many who could still receive it. The reason it is overlooked is because they may not be required to file a tax return. Here are some things you should know about EITC.

- ➢ Eligibility is limited to low-to-moderate income earners
- ➢ Self-employed still counts
- ➢ Investment income can disqualify you
- ➢ Eligibility fluctuates
- ➢ Tax software can help
- ➢ It is possible to lose EITC by being dishonest

Job Expenses: Keep in mind, if your job expenses exceed 2% of your income, you can itemize these deductions, although not all expenses can be deducted such as your daily lunch or items that are reimbursed by your employer. Here are some items you can deduct.

- ➢ Uniforms
- ➢ Professional dues
- ➢ Protective gear
- ➢ Safety equipment
- ➢ Small tools
- ➢ Costs associated with job hunting

Relocation Expenses: When you need to move based on your job, then you may be able to deduct those moving expenses. The same goes if you find a job in a new city and you need to move for the job. To claim this deduction, remember this:

- ➢ **Distance Test:** Your new workplace must be no less than 50 miles further from your residence than your old job was.
- ➢ **Time Test:** When you are the employee, it is required that you are full-time for 39 weeks of the first 12 months. This starts after you arrive in the location of the new workplace. Although

if you are self-employed it is the same with one addition. You must also work 78 weeks during your first 24 months.

Keep in mind, there are exceptions to the rule. For example, if you are in the military or have a death or disability that stops you from working. If you do qualify $0.23 per mile can be deducted. Also, if you need to move all of your household belongs and get a hotel for the nights of travel these are deductible too. You can check out the IRS publication 521 for additional information.

Education Tax Incentives: If you plan on going to college or have someone in your household who is attending college, you may want to pay attention to this credit. There are three tax incentives that are offered by the government.

- ➤ American Opportunity Tax Credit
- ➤ Lifetime Learning Credit
- ➤ Tuition and Fees Deduction

Check out the American Opportunity Tax Credit. Out of all three, this is the one that will give you the biggest return. With up to 40% of the credit refundable, you can get about $2,500 per year per student who is eligible.

How Can You Maximize Your Tax Deductions?

How many times you have filed taxes without seeing much of a return? Don't worry, you are not alone. There are millions of people who do not know how to make the IRS work for them. What are some basic things we can do to know and understand what we can do so IRS does not seem like the bad guy? When you think about it, taxes should not be thought of only at tax season. With a little planning, you can put yourself in a position for the greatest return by maximizing your tax deductions.

I want you to think about what I am about to say. You can claim a deduction for many of your payments that relate to your home, business and other miscellaneous expenses. It just takes proper planning. Let's go over a few things that will set you on the right track to maximizing your deductions and give you the greatest return. Don't worry, they are easy, and you will wonder why you did not think of it sooner.

Planning your mortgage payments: The interest you pay on your mortgage payment is deductible. Now if you plan it right you can increase your deduction. For example, if you prepay your January 2018 mortgage in December 2017, you will be able to deduct the extra payment in your taxes when you file. Remember this, the IRS does not care when the due date is. They care about when you make the payment.

Keep record of your interest payments on your mortgage: This is simple. For any payments you make; keep record. This is to include any forms of payments. Make sure your lender provides you a statement at the end of the year of all the interest and payments you made throughout the year. This should have a breakdown showing the totals and how much was applied to the interest. This is very important as only the interest is deductible and not the payments.

For large expenses get a home equity loan: If you have irregular purchases, need a large amount of money or are making renovations in your home, you should take out a home equity loan. By securing the loan with your home it sets you in a category that makes it so you can claim the interest payments. From a tax standpoint this is much better than an unsecured loan or a credit card loan.

Use a Schedule A to report your home mortgage payments: Make sure you are using the form 1040 (schedule A) to report your mortgage interest payments when you file taxes.

You can earn a tax credit for energy efficiency improvements: Want to save money throughout the year with energy efficient improvements? You will not only save money with these improvements, but you can also get a 30% tax credit for the improvements that are made. These are improvements such as a solar electric system, solar water heaters, fuel cells, small wind energy systems and geothermal heat pumps.

> ➢ To keep track of the allowable credit, you need to fill out the IRS form 5695 and the amount will be entered in line 53 of the 1040 tax return.

> ➢ Keep in mind, a deduction will reduce the taxable income while a credit is a direct reduction of how much tax you will owe.

Know Your Deductions & Your Exemptions: It is important to do the research and know what deductions and exemptions you may qualify for. Do your research and find out what you can claim. Do not start to figure this out only when it is time to file your taxes. Start in January and plan your year accordingly. This will help you set yourself up for a bigger return.

Build Your Retirement: A great way to maximize your deductions is through a company sponsored 401(k). If you have your own personal 401(k) that is great too. Make active contributions to it. This will help to lower your taxable income each year.

Use a Flexible Spending Account to pay for Medical Expenses: This kind of spending account is great. It allows you to set aside a portion of your pay towards medical expenses and child or dependent care. This is a pre-tax account.

Medical Cost Deductions: If you have a lot of medical expenses that are out of pocket, this is a great deduction. You can claim your medical bills throughout the year, to include health insurance premiums, dental care, eye care and glasses, mental health counseling and driving to and from the doctor for those appointments.

Donate to Charity: I am sure many of us have a closet full of things that you need to dust off once a year and that is the only time you look at them. Why not donate them or give a contribution to charity? The great thing is it could be tax-deductible. To claim them on your taxes you will use the Schedule A form and itemize your deductions.

I know these deductions look like they are centralized toward the individual tax payer. That is because these are. However, that does not mean they do not apply to a small business. It is important to know and understand the deductions and credits for both your employees and you as the employer and your business in general.

The key to staying ahead of the IRS with all their fees and audits will be outstanding record keeping. As you are tracking your expenses I want you to keep a few things in mind for your tracker. Remember, record keeping is essential. This is a great way to make those IRS audits seem easy.

Automobile Expenses: If you use your car for business purposes you can deduct the mileage, parking fee and tolls. Even though it is easier to take the standard deduction, it does not mean it gives you the biggest return. In fact, keeping a good track of the expenses for the car and itemizing them to be exact will give you the greatest return. This is to include repairs, insurance, maintenance and depreciation based of the business portion used. Keep in mind, if you are taking out a loan to purchase a car for the business, you can claim the interest paid on that loan. The same goes if you lease a car for the business; you can then claim the leasing cost.

Equipment, Furniture and Supplies: I advise, do not go out and buy equipment or furniture just so you can get a tax deduction. If you are thinking like this, you are doing it wrong and it is poor business sense. However, if you need the furniture, equipment or supplies for your business then go ahead and claim the deduction. This way you have equipment you can use while getting a great deduction.

Startup Business Expenses: It often takes a lot for a business to launch. That can mean a lot of expenses on your part. If you have any professional or legal expenses associated with the startup you will want to deduct those expenses over a 60-month period. You will also want to deduct the expenses from your startup during the first year. If you do not, then the deductions would be nondeductible until you sell or liquidate your business.

Home Office: If you have a home office, you may be able to deduct it on your business taxes. Keep in mind that there are some requirements. The room that you use must be strictly for your home office. That means it cannot act as a toy room, spare bedroom or anything else outside of the business. Although, it is worth having a home office. This will allow you to deduct a portion of rent, utilities, insurance, taxes, maintenance, professional cleaning, depreciation and interest. This also includes home and mobile phone. If it is used for business, you can only deduct the portion that is used for the business.

Employing your Spouse or Child: As a small business owner with employees, you are aware that you can deduct the salaries of your employees. This is to include if you employ your spouse or child. However, they will need to meet the same requirements as your regular employees. Remember this, just saying your family are employees does not qualify you for a deduction. They will need to meet the following conditions for your business to claim them as a deduction.

➢ You need to pay your child or spouse a salary.

➢ The salary you pay your child or spouse needs to be the same as you would pay a regular employee to do the same job.

> When paying your child, make sure it is a reasonable salary for the age of the child.

> The child or spouse must do the work necessary for the business. Which means, they need to be doing the same work as any employee to earn their salary.

Calculations for Tax-Deductible Business Expenses and Refunds

When you are ready to prepare and file your taxes for your small business, look at this checklist. This gives you a pretty extensive list to think about so you can get the best return for your business.

> **Income**

   o Keep your gross receipts from a sales or services.

   o For accrual-based taxpayers you will need to keep all sales records.

   o Include all returns and allowances.

   o Get a statement from your bank on your business checking/savings accounts showing your interest through the year (1009-INT or a statement).

   o Any other income that you bring in as a business.

> **Cost of Goods Sold (if applicable)**

   o Cost of your inventory for each item.

   o Your total beginning inventory dollar amount.

   o Any inventory you purchased.

   o The total ending inventory dollar amount.

   o Any items taken from the inventory for personal purposes.

   o Your materials and supplies.

- ➢ **Expenses**
  - ○ Advertising
  - ○ Phones (landline, fax and cell phones related to the business)
  - ○ Computer and internet expenses
  - ○ Transportation and travel expenses
    - ▪ Local transportation
      - • Business trip (mileage) log
      - • Contemporaneous log or receipts for public transportation, parking and tolls.
    - ▪ Travel away from home
      - • Airfare or mileage/actual expense if you drive
      - • Hotel
      - • Meals and Tips
      - • Taxis and Tips
      - • Internet connection (hotel, internet café, etc.)
      - • Other
  - ○ Commissions Paid to Subcontractors
    - ▪ File IRS form 1099-MISC and a IRS form 1096 as necessary
  - ○ Depreciation
    - ▪ The cost and the first date the business used the assets
    - ▪ Any records related to personal use of assets
    - ▪ The sales price and disposition date of any assets sold
  - ○ Business Insurance

- Casualty loss insurance
- Errors and Omissions
- Other
- Interest Expenses
  - Your mortgage interest on any buildings that are business owned
  - Interest on Business Loans
  - Investment expenses and interest
- Professional Fees
  - Lawyers, accountants and consultants
- Office Supplies
  - Pens, paper, staples and other consumables
- Rent Expense
  - Office space you rent
  - Business-use vehicle lease expense
  - Other
- Office-In-Home
  - Square footage of your home office space
  - Total square footage of your home
  - If you operate a day care, what are the hours you use the home and how many
  - Any mortgage interest or rent paid
  - Your homeowner's or renters' insurance
  - Your utilities

- Cost of home, separate improvements and first date of use for your business
  - Wages Paid to Employees
    - All IRS forms W-2s and W-3s
    - Federal and State Payroll returns (IRS forms 940, 941, etc.)
      - Employee benefit expenses (will need to be aligned to the left with "Wages paid to employees")
      - Contractors
      - IRS form 1099-MISC
      - IRS form 1096
  - Other Expenses
    - Any repairs, maintenance of office facility, etc.
    - Estimated tax payments that you have made
    - Other business-related expenses
      - Health Insurance (needs to be aligned to the left with "Other expenses")
      - Premiums paid to cover the sole-proprietor and family
      - Premiums paid on behalf of partners and S corporation shareholders
      - Information on spouse's employers provided insurance

I know this seems like an extensive list. However, this list will help you prepare for tax time. Do not only look at this list when it is time to see your accountant for filing your taxes. You should be looking at it throughout the year and preparing all year to bring in the maximum refund for your business.

Chapter 4 – Capital Gains and Losses

Every small business must worry about capital gains and losses. There are really two main reason a business will see one or the other. When you have sold a capital asset, you see a capital gain or loss. his can be as a company or individual, which brings us to one of the ways a business may experience a gain or loss. Now let's look at the two ways.

1. When you have sold a product or service you may make a profit on that sale or a loss of money if you spent more on the asset than you got from the sale.

2. Many times, you may have an investment in items that the business owns, and you sell those items to make room for new equipment. By doing this you may make a profit if you are able to sale the equipment for more than you originally purchased it for. However, if you calculate wear and tear and sell it at a price below the market value you could take a loss for that equipment.

It is important that you understand that each one is taxed differently with the IRS. Your business profits will be taxed as ordinary income, which will be at the regular business or individual tax rate based on how you have your small business set up.

Now when it is a gain or loss from an investment or sale of a business asset then it is also taxed as a capital gain or loss. Remember, a capital gain is when your business writes off a business asset and then takes it off the balance sheet.

Most everything you use for your business can be considered as a capital asset when it is used as an investment. When you have a business owner or investor who sells their shares in the business, they will also experience a capital gain or loss of the sales of your capital assets. It is important to remember that capital gains and losses are different than your operating gains and losses. Therefore, make sure to keep them straight and know the difference between them.

> **Operating Gains and Losses:** As you receive profit from day-to-day operations you are receiving operating gains. Although, if you experience a loss in the daily operations then it is an operating loss. For tax purposes your operating loss may be called Net Operating Losses (NOL).

> **Capital Gains and Losses:** These gains and losses result from single transactions that will bring a business gain or loss. There are two types of capital gains and losses.

o Short-Term Capital Gains and Losses: These are held for one year or less before they are sold.

o Long-Term Capital Gains and Losses: These are held for more than one year and then sold.

Most people overlook the power that comes with capital gains and losses. I say this because if you want to maximize your tax return, it is vital that you understand them and how they work.

When it comes to capital gains you need to figure out how much your assets are worth and how much you purchased them for. This will include stocks, bonds, funds, collectibles such as artwork and anything your business considers as an asset. Then if you have sold it, how much did you sell for? If you sold it above the price you purchased it for then you made a profit. However, if you sold an item for less than its value and less than what you purchased it for you will experience a loss.

Whenever you make a gain on your investment you must pay taxes on that gain. However, if you take a loss you can claim your losses on your tax return. You can use this to your advantage by cutting your gain to a small margin and pay a lower amount in taxes.

When you report your capital gains and losses it will be on a schedule D (Capital Gains and Losses) and a form 8949 (Sales and Other Dispositions of Capital Assets).

Helpful Facts to Know

As we learn about capital gains and loss, here are a few helpful tips and facts that will help you along in your quest for understanding this vital area.

- ➤ **Capital Assets:** These assets will include property such as a home or a car and investments such as stocks and bonds.

- ➤ **Gains and Losses:** These are the differences between your investment and the amount you receive from the sale.

- ➤ **Net Investment Income Tax:** All capital gains taken as income are subject to this tax if your income reaches above a specific amount. Check out the IRS website for the most current rates.

- ➤ **Deductible Losses:** When you are selling an investment property and take a loss on that sale you can deduct that loss. However, if you take a loss on property you sold for personal use you cannot make that deduction.

- ➤ **Limit on Losses:** Keep this in mind; if you have a capital loss that is more than your capital gain you can deduct the difference on your tax return as a loss.

- ➤ **Carryover Losses:** When you have a capital loss more than the limit you can deduct in that year, you can carry over the rest of the loss onto next year's taxes.

- ➢ **Long and Short Term:** Depending on how long you hold the asset before selling it can be consider long-term or short-term.

- ➢ **Net Capital Gain:** If you have long-term gains more than the losses, the difference will the net capital gain. he same with the short-term gains verses the short-term losses.

- ➢ **Tax Rate:** This will usually depend on the income from the business.

- ➢ **Forms to File:** There are a few forms you will need to remember.

  - o Form 8949 – Sales and Other Dispositions of Capital Assets (must file)

  - o Form 1040 Schedule D – Capital Gains and Losses (must file)

- o Form 8960 – Net Investment Income Tax-Individuals, Estates and Trust (file if qualify)

Capital Gains and Losses Computation

One key aspect of gains and losses are the computations. You need to figure out how much of a capital gain or loss you will need to record from your assets. This process is considered the netting process. It considers all gains and losses from both long-term and short-term points.

Step one: You will need to figure out your short-term gains and losses. These would be considered your capital assets that were sold or exchanged with one year or less.

- ➢ Add up all your short-term gains.

- ➢ Add up all your short-term losses.

- Subtract the total short-term losses from the total short-term gains (S/T losses – S/T gains).
  - If your short-term gains are greater than your short-term losses, then you have a net short-term gain.
  - If your short-term losses are greater than your short-term gains, then you have a net short-term loss.

Step two: Now we need to figure out the long-term gains and losses. Keep in mind that these are the gains and losses that will consist of the capital assets sold or exchanged over one year.

- Add up all your long-term gains.
- Add up all your long-term losses.
- Subtract the total long-term losses from the total long-term gains (L/T losses – L/T gains).
  - If your long-term gains are greater than your long-term losses, then you have a net long-term gain.
  - If your long-term losses are greater than your long-term gains, then you have a net long-term loss.

Step 3: Great! Now that you have your totals for short-term and long-term gains and losses it is time to add them up. There are different scenarios for each one and I will list them here for your convenience.

- When you have a net gain in short-term and long-term:
  - Your net short-term gain will be taxed at the ordinary income tax rate.
  - Your net long-term gain will be taxed at a lower capital gain rate.
- When you have a net short-term gain and a net long-term loss:

- When you have a net short-term gain that is greater than the net long-term loss then it will be taxed at the ordinary tax rate.

- When you have a net long-term loss that is greater than the short-term gain then you can deduct up to $3,000 of the loss on your form 1040 on line 13 under other income. However, if your loss is greater than $3,000 you can carry it over to next year's taxes. Make sure you remember to keep a record of your losses that are carried over for preparing your next year's return.

➢ When you have a net short-term loss and a net long-term gain:

- When you have a long-term gain that is greater than your short-term loss, you will have a net long-term gain and it will be taxed at the lower capital gain rate.

- When you have a short-term loss that is greater than your long-term gain there will be a net short-term loss. These are considered a net short-term loss. However, if your loss is greater than $3,000 you can carry it over to next year's taxes. Make sure you remember to keep a record of your losses that are carried over for preparing your next year's return.

➢ When you have a net short-term loss and a net long-term loss:

- You can deduct up to $3,000 of the losses and recorded on form 1040 on line 13. Any amount that is over $3,000 can be carried over to next year's taxes for both short-term and long-term losses.

- Make sure you keep record of what amounts are over the $3,000 limits and keep the short-term and long-term losses separate. This will be used in the calculations with the gains and losses for the next year's taxes.

- o Now if your short-term losses are less than the $3,000 limit, you can deduct your long-term losses to meet that limit and carry the rest over to the next year's taxes.

Capital Expenses and Depreciation

Almost every company has capital assets. Some of these assets, such as vehicles, will depreciate or lose value over time. That means you need to consider the value of its useful life and calculate the depreciation of the asset. Another example of an asset that will depreciate over time would be buildings.

Granted these assets depreciate, they are considered capital expenditure assets. That means the funds from the company are used to purchase them. Capital expenditure funds can also be used for upgrades, maintenance of property, industrial buildings and equipment such as an office and vehicles. Usually these expenses are used for special business projects and investments.

One thing to remember about depreciation: if its useful life is greater than one year, it will be depreciated. It will allow for businesses to write-off any losses that was due to wear and tear of the asset.

There are a few things to consider when you are calculating capital expenses and depreciation.

- ➢ To calculate capital expenditures (CapEx):
  - o You can add the total depreciation for the current year, so it will change the amount of the fixed asset.
    - ▪ Formula: CapEx = PP&E (current) – PP&E (prior) + Depreciation

- o During the measurement period this will be the total amount the business spent on the capital expenditures.
- ➢ To calculate depreciation; you have several ways to do it. However, I am not going to go through every way available. I want to keep it simple:
  - o The Straight-line method is the easiest way to calculate depreciation.
    - ▪ Formula: Annual Depreciation Expense = (Asset Cost – Residual Value) / Useful Life of the Asset
  - o To keep it simple. You need the following information for the calculation:
    - ▪ Cost of Asset
    - ▪ Residual Value
    - ▪ Useful Life
- ➢ As I mentioned, there are several ways to calculate depreciation. Here is a list of the different options that will give you various results. However, if you start using one then use the same one for all your depreciations so it will be accurate.
  - o Double Declining Balance Method
  - o Annuity Depreciation
  - o Sum-Of-Years-Digits Method
  - o Units-Of-Production Depreciation Method
  - o Units of Time Depreciation
  - o Group Depreciation Method
  - o Composite Depreciation Method

Through capital expenditures to depreciation ratios, the investors of your business can see how healthy your business is. This makes for good business judgements and decisions for moving forward.

Since improvements and upgrades to your assets are for furthering your business and considered capital expenditures, they cannot be deducted on your tax return. However, they do depreciate. Based off the depreciation associated with your business, they can be deducted on your taxes. Remember, capital gain expenses cannot be deducted, but the depreciation of those capital gains can be deducted.

Chapter 5 – Your Business and the IRS

It does not matter if you are an individual or a business owner, the IRS can seem a bit intimidating. They are known for their strict regulations and policies to ensure everyone is following the federal tax laws. Do not let them scare you as their website includes everything you need to know about the tax policies as well as the forms you need.

Avoid Problems with the IRS

I know none of us want any problems with the IRS. Even though they can seem relentless in the audits and investigations, there are a few simple things you can do to avoid the harsh punishments of Uncle Sam's relentless squad. Think of it this way, the IRS gives the toughest test you will ever take. However, they provide an entire website with all the answers.

File Taxes on Time: The IRS does not like it if you do not file your taxes on time or don't do it at all. It raises suspicions and you are bound to be audited. Make sure you are aware of the filing deadlines to avoid fees and penalties for filing late. This will also speed up the process of receiving your returns and allowing you to focus on your business. Make sure the IRS does not think you are earning money illegally. Yes, if you do not file your taxes at all, this is exactly what they will start thinking.

Report All Sources of Income: If you have multiple sources of income, you must report all sources. This includes any cash payments that were not taxed by the government and your estimated expenses. Before you file all your income sources, be sure to check and make sure the amounts are accurate. If during the initial filing or follow up audits there is any deviation, it will raise some red flags and questions from the IRS will follow.

When the IRS Talks, Respond Promptly: When you receive any communication from the IRS, do not sit on it and do nothing. Always read any communication from the IRS. If they are asking for some type of action, you need to comply within the given deadline. If you ignore the communication, it will raise the suspicions.

If You Owe It, Pay It: Keep in mind that if you pay what you owe to the IRS upon the first request you will not need to live in fear of them. If you have a legitimate reason for not being able to pay in full, call the IRS and speak to an agent. They will most likely be happy to help you create a payment plan. They may be strict but are willing to help. It is when you do not contact them and make arrangements that problems with the IRS start to arise.

Do Not Lie: This is easy. Be honest with the IRS regarding your taxes. If you knowingly withhold your information from the IRS, you are looking for trouble. As long as you report your income and all sources and number of dependents correctly, as well as business operations and anything else required from the IRS, you will not have any issues.

Hire a Tax Preparation Specialist: If you want to ensure that there will not be any problems with the IRS, you may want to hire a tax specialist. They specialize in keeping up with the tax laws. This means that if there are any issues with the IRS, the specialist will be held partially responsible.

Record Keeping is the Key to Success

Keeping good records is an essential part of your business. This not only helps with IRS and your taxes, but it also helps you to make good business decisions to thrust your business into the future. The records you keep will help monitor your business progression, prepare financial statements, identify where your income is coming from, prepare your tax returns and act as supporting documents for the things you claim on your tax return.

I am sure you are wondering what things you should keep a record of. These are just the minimum that should be kept. Although, a good rule to live by is "when in doubt, keep it."

➢ Banking information such as bank transactions and bank statements.

➢ Proof of income, such as anything from services rendered to sales made. Keep in mind, if you are given an invoice for payment, you should keep it.

➢ Expenses that you may have such as utilities, mortgage, rent, etc. You should keep the receipts of all the things you've purchased for business use.

➢ Your cash books, which keeps a record of the business transactions. This is showing what your money is doing for the business.

➢ Your wage books to show how much you pay your employees as well as records of all withholdings.

Make sure you keep these records organized. Along with these types of items, you should also keep any records that will be associated with the creation of your business and everything in between. Keeping a hard copy is important and having it organized is just as important. Another thing that helps is to keep the files on the cloud. That means, scan all your documents and keep them organized on a business cloud sharing platform. Organize and label them the same as you do the hard copies. This way it makes it easy to find the physical copy when you need to. By having all your documents already scanned into the cloud-based platform, it will allow you to quickly send them to the IRS if they need them for an audit. It will also allow you to get them to your accountant easily by allowing them to have access to the platform and folders.

The main items your account will need access to for your tax records will be:

> Sales

> Income

> Expenses

> Assets

> Liabilities

With all these records, you will almost need to have a separate filing room. If your business has been around for 20 years, that would be a long time to keep your records and you will or have already run out of space. So, how long do you need to keep these records? Due to the IRS being able to conduct audits several years later, you will need to keep all your records for a standard time frame.

> A standard time is to keep your records for three years since the date you filed your tax return or two years from the date you paid your taxes. It will be determined based on which date is the longest when you file for a claim of credit or refund after you file your return.

> If you file a claim that has a loss from worthless securities or a bad debt deduction you will need to keep your records for seven years.

> If you do not report income that should have been reported and that income was more than 25% of your gross income on your return, you will need to keep your records for six years.

> If you never filed the return, you will need to keep your records indefinitely.

> If you file a fraudulent return, you will need to keep your records indefinitely.

> For all employment tax records, you should keep them for four years after the date the tax was due or is paid, depending on which date is later.

Sometimes the hardest part is knowing which records to keep. There are some basic questions you can ask yourself that will help you decide. However, when in doubt, keep it.

> Are the records connected to property?

  o Keep records pertaining to property until the period of limitations expires. This is based off the year you disposed the property.

  o These records need to be kept for calculating depreciation, amortization or depletion deductions to figure out any gains or losses when you sell or dispose the property.

> What should I do with my records of nontax purpose?

  o If you no longer need the records for tax purposes, do not discard them. Check to make sure you do not need them for any other purposes before discarding them.

There are three easy steps that will help you with better business record keeping. These will help you get organized and stay organized. Your records are key to your success.

> **Know exactly what you need to record:** Every business needs to file a tax return. Knowing what records to keep are half the battle. They will show you the profits and losses of the company.

  o **Invoices:** These will keep a record of all your income. It is important to know what transactions bring in a profit for the business. There is some basic information that needs to be on each invoice such as:

    ▪ Description of the job performed

- Date job was completed
- Company address with phone number and company name (logo or branding)
- Registration number
- Invoice number

o **Receipts:** Keeping track of your expenses is crucial. Keep your receipts for everything the business spends money on. These receipts can be for a variety of things such as the following:

- Work travel
- Business lunches
- Office space
- Supplies

o **Other:** There are other items that your business may need to keep a record of. This is based on the needs of your business.

- Cashbooks
- Bank Statements
- Wage Books

➢ **Get the Right Apps:** To simplify things for you, your business and your accountant should aim to work with excellent apps. You do not need to spend much on these. In fact, some are free, and they work just as well. Many apps offer some great features that will help you with your record keeping such as scanning invoices and receipts in the accounting software you choose. If you use a cloud-based software, it is easy for you to give permission for others to access it and work remotely on your business taxes, finances and record keeping.

> **Separate your Business and Personal Finances:** Always separate your personal and business finances. That is to include having a separate bank account for the business. Keeping your finances separate will make it easier to file your tax returns for the business and yourself. This will help you keep track of all transactions made by the company.

Survival Guide for an IRS Audit and Your Rights

Audits by the IRS can be scary. However, you can survive them and make it through an IRS Audit without any issues. Throughout this book we have discussed many things for filing your taxes. In a way, you are reading a survival guide. However, the IRS has a set of rules that could make it hard on your business if not followed. As we've just talked about, record keeping is key to your success. Here I will show you why having these records are so important and how get through an audit by the IRS with ease.

Don't Ignore an IRS Audit: The worst thing you can do is ignore a letter from the IRS. If you do, they will think something is wrong and it will be harder on you and your business. They will go through everything thinking you got something to hide. Trust me, if you are hiding something, they will find it. Simply reply to the IRS and comply with what they need for your audit or the instructions in the letter. Make sure you follow all instructions you are given in the notice.

They generally give you 30 days to respond to the notice. The terms will be outlined in the notice you receive. Keep in mind, if you do not respond and ignore the notice, the IRS can act and adjust your tax liability. That means the next time they send you a notice it will be a bill instead. Now it just cost your business money because you did not reply to the notice.

Have your Records Organized: Keep all your records organized. This will make the job of the audit easier. The best part is, it will win you points with the IRS. It shows them you are a professional and you take pride in your business. Trust me, if they ask for documents and you just give it to them in an unorganized manner, the IRS will go deeper and work harder on your audit. If your records are organized, they may not work as hard and will finish a lot faster. If there are discrepancies, it is your job to prove yourself and clear your name to make things right.

If it is missing, replace it: While you are preparing for an audit and you find some records missing, get them replaced before the audit. Never go into the audit claiming they are lost or missing. If you do this, it would not matter how organized your records are. The IRS will think you are unorganized. Two scenarios could happen if you are missing the records.

➢ The auditor may request that you obtain the record and give you a time to do so.

➢ The auditor may consider that the document is missing and deny the claim that the record supports.

Only bring the documents asked for: You do not need to bring your entire room of files. The IRS does not need everything. Only bring what is asked for. If it is not asked for then leave it. If the auditor asked about something that was not listed in the instructions of the audit notice, you can politely let them know that those records are in the office records and was not asked for in the notice. Unless it is a pressing matter, the issue will usually be dropped, and they will not ask for more.

Give the auditor respect: Be respectful to the auditor. They have a family just like you and are just doing their job. Remember, if you give them issues, they can make it harder on you and your business.

Always provide copies only: Never give your originals to the auditor. If you do bring the originals, ask the auditor to make copies and give the originals back. If you give them the originals, there will be a good chance they are misplaced or lost. Remember, this your business. These documents are part of that great business you have established.

Stay on point: Through a simple discussion, the auditor can get some valuable information about who you are and your business. Know what is in your records and stay alert to what the auditor is asking. If you can answer with a simple yes or no, then do it. This will keep you from saying things that could hurt you in the audit. Do not give the auditor a reason to expand your audit due to ramblings and bad tendencies.

Be prepared: Throughout the audit process, if the IRS sees a credit or deduction you should not have gotten, be prepared to pay for any penalties that are imposed. They can add interest on unpaid penalties. Therefore, it is best to be prepared to pay them if any are given.

Claiming Your Previous Years' Tax Deductions

You may wonder if you are able to claim your tax deductions from previous years. The simple answer is that you cannot claim the previous years' tax deductions. However, there are some things you should be aware of with claiming the previous years' deductions. An example are business losses, they can be claimed on the next year's return if your previous year's loss was over $3,000.

For those who have made charitable deductions and it exceeded the limit for that year's deduction, you can carry over the contribution amount that could not be claimed. For the most part, you can only claim the deductions made during the current year. That means, if you did not file your return, you run the risk of losing any refund that you may have received. However, you can file the return as a separate return within three years to still be eligible for any refund you may receive. If it is after three years, you forfeit and file a return on your taxes.

Keep in mind, if you forgot any deduction on a previous years' return, you cannot claim that deduction on your current return. However, you can submit an amendment to the previous year's return.

Chapter 6 – Making Your Business Taxes Work for You

There are many levels of taxes you should be aware of. Knowing what types are available will help you to learn how you can make them work for you.

Personal Income Tax: Most states now require you to pay a personal income tax. They usually use one of two different methods to determine this. You have the graduated income tax and the flat rate income tax. Regardless of how your state determines which rate to use, the taxpayer needs to figure out what their taxable income will be.

State Sales Tax: This is based on the sale of goods and services. Most of the time it is set by paying sales tax when you purchase items. It can be categorized into three different areas.

> **Vendor Tax:** This is a tax system that taxes the person who is doing business. It is imposed by some states as the businesspeople are considered to having a privilege when doing business in the state. The tax is based on goods sold.

> **Consumer Tax:** This is a tax system that taxes the retail sale. That means the vendor collects the tax from the buyers and send that tax money to the state.

> **Combination:** This is a tax system that taxes the vendor who is then required to pass the tax onto the consumer. If you are the consumer, it will look identical to a consumer states tax.

Property Tax: The revenue from property tax usually goes towards financing public services. These types of services are public schools, police protection, sanitation, etc. This can change based on the state. Each state may have a different rate.

Other State Taxes: Each state is different, and you should check with your state for all the taxes that are imposed. Here are just a few to consider.

> ➢ **Fuel Tax:** It does not matter what state you are in, there is a fuel tax that is imposed. That means that when you buy gasoline or diesel fuel, it is cents-per-gallon tax. It does vary from state to state. However, the concept is the same.

> ➢ **Inheritance and Estate Taxes:** When you transfer property after someone has died, you will see an inheritance tax. With this tax system, the beneficiary must pay the tax on the property. With the same concept, estate is slightly different. This tax is based on the entire estate of the individual.

> ➢ **Corporate Income Tax:** This tax is imposed by most states and may be at a lower income tax rate as part of the business incentives. These incentives are designed to encourage businesses to operate in their state.

Business Taxes and You

We talked a lot about taxes and the IRS. It is time to take all your hard work and make it work for you. Many businesses work as a pass-through business. That means the profits will pass through the business directly to the owner's return. Then the owner pays the taxes on the income. These types of businesses usually are sole proprietorships, partnerships, limited liability companies (LLC) and S corporations.

Sometimes your business will take on an administrative tax burden. These burdens could hurt your business, if you allow it to. Although, how can you make these work for you? Simple, use them as a learning experience and use brainstorming to come up with ideas you can do to increase sales and profit for your business. Claim these burdens onto your taxes and turn them around over time. By claiming simple things such as a capital loss on your tax return, you can get a return on your taxes to put back into the pockets of the business.

Chapter 7 – Forms for Success

As promised, I am including a special bonus of the forms that will help as a guide to your business tax filing. Keep in mind that some of these forms do have the year printed on the form. Make sure you are using the most current form when filing them. The IRS will not accept the forms if it is the wrong edition.

You will find a brief explanation of each form and a picture of the form for each one. It is important that you know how to fill out each form completely. I will give some basic information but to get a more thorough explanation of the form you can google search for each form.

IRS Form 940 – Employer's Annual Federal Unemployment (FUTA) Tax Return

A business will use the IRS Form 940 to compute the federal unemployment tax liability of the previous year. It will also be used to show the amount of unemployment tax owed and how much is unpaid.

Form 940 for 2017: Employer's Annual Federal Unemployment (FUTA) Tax Return

Department of the Treasury — Internal Revenue Service

850113

OMB No. 1545-0028

Employer identification number (EIN)

Name (not your trade name)

Trade name (if any)

Address

Number   Street   Suite or room number

City   State   ZIP code

Foreign country name   Foreign province/county   Foreign postal code

Type of Return
(Check all that apply.)

- [ ] a. Amended
- [ ] b. Successor employer
- [ ] c. No payments to employees in 2017
- [ ] d. Final: Business closed or stopped paying wages

Go to www.irs.gov/Form940 for instructions and the latest information.

Read the separate instructions before you complete this form. Please type or print within the boxes.

Part 1: Tell us about your return. If any line does NOT apply, leave it blank. See instructions before completing Part 1.

1a If you had to pay state unemployment tax in one state only, enter the state abbreviation . 1a [ ] [ ]

1b If you had to pay state unemployment tax in more than one state, you are a multi-state employer . . . . 1b [ ] Check here. Complete Schedule A (Form 940).

2 If you paid wages in a state that is subject to CREDIT REDUCTION . . . . 2 [ ] Check here. Complete Schedule A (Form 940).

Part 2: Determine your FUTA tax before adjustments. If any line does NOT apply, leave it blank.

3 Total payments to all employees . . . . 3 [   ]

4 Payments exempt from FUTA tax . . . . 4 [   ]

Check all that apply: 4a [ ] Fringe benefits   4c [ ] Retirement/Pension   4e [ ] Other
                       4b [ ] Group-term life insurance   4d [ ] Dependent care

5 Total of payments made to each employee in excess of $7,000 . . . . 5 [   ]

6 Subtotal (line 4 + line 5 = line 6) . . . . 6 [   ]

7 Total taxable FUTA wages (line 3 – line 6 = line 7). See instructions . . . . 7 [   ]

8 FUTA tax before adjustments (line 7 x 0.006 = line 8) . . . . 8 [   ]

Part 3: Determine your adjustments. If any line does NOT apply, leave it blank.

9 If ALL of the taxable FUTA wages you paid were excluded from state unemployment tax, multiply line 7 by 0.054 (line 7 x 0.054 = line 9). Go to line 12 . . . . 9 [   ]

10 If SOME of the taxable FUTA wages you paid were excluded from state unemployment tax, OR you paid ANY state unemployment tax late (after the due date for filing Form 940), complete the worksheet in the instructions. Enter the amount from line 7 of the worksheet . . 10 [   ]

11 If credit reduction applies, enter the total from Schedule A (Form 940) . . . . . . 11 [   ]

Part 4: Determine your FUTA tax and balance due or overpayment. If any line does NOT apply, leave it blank.

12 Total FUTA tax after adjustments (lines 8 + 9 + 10 + 11 = line 12) . . . . 12 [   ]

13 FUTA tax deposited for the year, including any overpayment applied from a prior year . 13 [   ]

14 Balance due. If line 12 is more than line 13, enter the excess on line 14.
- If line 14 is more than $500, you must deposit your tax.
- If line 14 is $500 or less, you may pay with this return. See instructions . . . . 14 [   ]

15 Overpayment. If line 13 is more than line 12, enter the excess on line 15 and check a box below 15 [   ]
➤ You MUST complete both pages of this form and SIGN it.   Check one: [ ] Apply to next return.   [ ] Send a refund.

Next ➡

For Privacy Act and Paperwork Reduction Act Notice, see the back of the Payment Voucher.   Cat. No. 112340   Form **940** (2017)

850212

Name (not your trade name)

Employer identification number (EIN)

Part 5: Report your FUTA tax liability by quarter only if line 12 is more than $500. If not, go to Part 6.

16 Report the amount of your FUTA tax liability for each quarter; do NOT enter the amount you deposited. If you had no liability for a quarter, leave the line blank.

16a 1st quarter (January 1 – March 31) . . . . 16a [.]

16b 2nd quarter (April 1 – June 30) . . . . 16b [.]

16c 3rd quarter (July 1 – September 30) . . . . 16c [.]

16d 4th quarter (October 1 – December 31) . . . . 16d [.]

17 Total tax liability for the year (lines 16a + 16b + 16c + 16d = line 17) 17 [.] Total must equal line 12.

Part 6: May we speak with your third-party designee?

Do you want to allow an employee, a paid tax preparer, or another person to discuss this return with the IRS? See the instructions for details.

☐ Yes. Designee's name and phone number [   ] [   ]

Select a 5-digit Personal Identification Number (PIN) to use when talking to IRS [ ][ ][ ][ ][ ]

☐ No.

Part 7: Sign here. You MUST complete both pages of this form and SIGN it.

Under penalties of perjury, I declare that I have examined this return, including accompanying schedules and statements, and to the best of my knowledge and belief, it is true, correct, and complete, and that no part of any payment made to a state unemployment fund claimed as a credit was, or is to be, deducted from the payments made to employees. Declaration of preparer (other than taxpayer) is based on all information of which preparer has any knowledge.

✗ Sign your name here [   ] Print your name here [   ]

Print your title here [   ]

Date [/ /] Best daytime phone [   ]

Paid Preparer Use Only Check if you are self-employed ☐

Preparer's name [   ] PTIN [   ]

Preparer's signature [   ] Date [/ /]

Firm's name (or yours if self-employed) [   ] EIN [   ]

Address [   ] Phone [   ]

City [   ] State [   ] ZIP code [   ]

Form **940** (2017)

IRS Form 941 – Employer's Quarterly Federal Tax Return

Form 941 will be used when you need to inform the IRS quarterly regarding your federal withholding. This is important as it lets the IRS know what taxes have been taken out of each employee pay.

Form **941 for 2017:** Employer's QUARTERLY Federal Tax Return

(Rev. January 2017) Department of the Treasury — Internal Revenue Service

950117

OMB No. 1545-0029

Employer identification number (EIN) [ ][ ] - [ ][ ][ ][ ][ ][ ][ ]

Name (not your trade name)

Trade name (if any)

Address

Number   Street   Suite or room number

City   State   ZIP code

Foreign country name   Foreign province/county   Foreign postal code

Report for this Quarter of 2017
(Check one.)

☐ 1: January, February, March

☐ 2: April, May, June

☐ 3: July, August, September

☐ 4: October, November, December

Instructions and prior year forms are available at www.irs.gov/form941.

Read the separate instructions before you complete Form 941. Type or print within the boxes.

Part 1: Answer these questions for this quarter.

1   Number of employees who received wages, tips, or other compensation for the pay period including: Mar. 12 (Quarter 1), June 12 (Quarter 2), Sept. 12 (Quarter 3), or Dec. 12 (Quarter 4) 1 [   ]

2   Wages, tips, and other compensation . . . . 2 [.]

3   Federal income tax withheld from wages, tips, and other compensation . . . . . 3 [.]

4   If no wages, tips, and other compensation are subject to social security or Medicare tax ☐ Check and go to line 6.

		Column 1		Column 2
5a	Taxable social security wages . .	[.]	× 0.124 =	[.]
5b	Taxable social security tips . . .	[.]	× 0.124 =	[.]
5c	Taxable Medicare wages & tips. .	[.]	× 0.029 =	[.]
5d	Taxable wages & tips subject to Additional Medicare Tax withholding	[.]	× 0.009 =	[.]

5e   Add Column 2 from lines 5a, 5b, 5c, and 5d . . . . 5e [.]

5f   Section 3121(q) Notice and Demand—Tax due on unreported tips (see instructions) . . 5f [.]

6   Total taxes before adjustments. Add lines 3, 5e, and 5f . . . . 6 [.]

7   Current quarter's adjustment for fractions of cents . . . . 7 [.]

8   Current quarter's adjustment for sick pay . . . . 8 [.]

9   Current quarter's adjustments for tips and group-term life insurance . . . . . . 9 [.]

10   Total taxes after adjustments. Combine lines 6 through 9 . . . . 10 [.]

11   Qualified small business payroll tax credit for increasing research activities. Attach Form 8974 11 [.]

12   Total taxes after adjustments and credits. Subtract line 11 from line 10 . . . . 12 [.]

13   Total deposits for this quarter, including overpayment applied from a prior quarter and overpayments applied from Form 941-X, 941-X (PR), 944-X, or 944-X (SP) filed in the current quarter 13 [.]

14   Balance due. If line 12 is more than line 13, enter the difference and see instructions . . . 14 [.]

15   Overpayment. If line 13 is more than line 12, enter the difference [.] Check one: ☐ Apply to next return. ☐ Send a refund.

▶ You MUST complete both pages of Form 941 and SIGN it. Next ▶

For Privacy Act and Paperwork Reduction Act Notice, see the back of the Payment Voucher. Cat. No. 17001Z Form **941** (Rev. 1-2017)

Name (not your trade name)	Employer identification number (EIN)

Part 2: Tell us about your deposit schedule and tax liability for this quarter.

If you are unsure about whether you are a monthly schedule depositor or a semiweekly schedule depositor, see section 11 of Pub. 15.

16 Check one: ☐ Line 12 on this return is less than $2,500 or line 12 (line 10 if the prior quarter was the fourth quarter of 2016) on the return for the prior quarter was less than $2,500, and you didn't incur a $100,000 next-day deposit obligation during the current quarter. If line 12 (line 10 if the prior quarter was the fourth quarter of 2016) for the prior quarter was less than $2,500 but line 12 on this return is $100,000 or more, you must provide a record of your federal tax liability. If you are a monthly schedule depositor, complete the deposit schedule below; if you are a semiweekly schedule depositor, attach Schedule B (Form 941). Go to Part 3.

☐ **You were a monthly schedule depositor for the entire quarter.** Enter your tax liability for each month and total liability for the quarter, then go to Part 3.

Tax liability: Month 1 [.]

Month 2 [.]

Month 3 [.]

Total liability for quarter [.]   Total must equal line 12.

☐ **You were a semiweekly schedule depositor for any part of this quarter.** Complete Schedule B (Form 941), Report of Tax Liability for Semiweekly Schedule Depositors, and attach it to Form 941.

Part 3: Tell us about your business. If a question does NOT apply to your business, leave it blank.

17 If your business has closed or you stopped paying wages . . . . ☐ Check here, and

enter the final date you paid wages [/ /] .

18 If you are a seasonal employer and you don't have to file a return for every quarter of the year . . . ☐ Check here.

Part 4: May we speak with your third-party designee?

Do you want to allow an employee, a paid tax preparer, or another person to discuss this return with the IRS? See the instructions for details.

☐ Yes. Designee's name and phone number [ ] [ ]

Select a 5-digit Personal Identification Number (PIN) to use when talking to the IRS. ☐ ☐ ☐ ☐ ☐

☐ No.

Part 5: Sign here. You MUST complete both pages of Form 941 and SIGN it.

Under penalties of perjury, I declare that I have examined this return, including accompanying schedules and statements, and to the best of my knowledge and belief, it is true, correct, and complete. Declaration of preparer (other than taxpayer) is based on all information of which preparer has any knowledge.

X Sign your name here [ ]

Print your name here [ ]

Print your title here [ ]

Date [/ /]

Best daytime phone [ ]

Paid Preparer Use Only

Check if you are self-employed . . . ☐

Preparer's name	[ ]	PTIN	[ ]
Preparer's signature	[ ]	Date	[/ /]
Firm's name (or yours if self-employed)	[ ]	EIN	[ ]
Address	[ ]	Phone	[ ]
City	[ ] State [ ]	ZIP code	[ ]

Page 2

Form **941** (Rev. 1-2017)

Form 941-V,
Payment Voucher

Purpose of Form

Complete Form 941-V if you're making a payment with Form 941. We will use the completed voucher to credit your payment more promptly and accurately, and to improve our service to you.

Making Payments With Form 941

To avoid a penalty, make your payment with Form 941 only if:

• Your total taxes for either the current quarter (Form 941, line 12) or the preceding quarter (Form 941, line 12 (line 10 if the preceding quarter was the fourth quarter of 2016)) are less than $2,500, you didn't incur a $100,000 next-day deposit obligation during the current quarter, and you're paying in full with a timely filed return; or

• You are a monthly schedule depositor making a payment in accordance with the Accuracy of Deposits Rule. See section 11 of Pub. 15 for details. In this case, the amount of your payment may be $2,500 or more.

Otherwise, you must make deposits by electronic funds transfer. See section 11 of Pub. 15 for deposit instructions. Don't use Form 941-V to make federal tax deposits.

⚠ Use Form 941-V when making any payment with Form 941. However, if you pay an amount with Form 941 that should've been deposited, you may be subject to a penalty. See Deposit Penalties in section 11 of Pub. 15.

Specific Instructions

Box 1—Employer identification number (EIN). If you don't have an EIN, you may apply for one online by visiting the IRS website at www.irs.gov/ein. You may also apply for an EIN by faxing or mailing Form SS-4 to the IRS. If you haven't received your EIN by the due date of Form 941, write "Applied For" and the date you applied in this entry space.

Box 2—Amount paid. Enter the amount paid with Form 941.

Box 3—Tax period. Darken the circle identifying the quarter for which the payment is made. Darken only one circle.

Box 4—Name and address. Enter your name and address as shown on Form 941.

• Enclose your check or money order made payable to "United States Treasury." Be sure to enter your EIN, "Form 941," and the tax period ("1st Quarter 2017," "2nd Quarter 2017," "3rd Quarter 2017," or "4th Quarter 2017") on your check or money order. Don't send cash. Don't staple Form 941-V or your payment to Form 941 (or to each other).

• Detach Form 941-V and send it with your payment and Form 941 to the address in the Instructions for Form 941.

Note: You must also complete the entity information above Part 1 on Form 941.

✂ ▼ **Detach Here and Mail With Your Payment and Form 941.** ▼ ✂

Form **941-V**		**Payment Voucher**	OMB No. 1545-0029
Department of the Treasury Internal Revenue Service		▶ Don't staple this voucher or your payment to Form 941.	**2017**

1 Enter your employer identification number (EIN).		2 Enter the amount of your payment. ▶ Make your check or money order payable to "United States Treasury"	Dollars	Cents

3 Tax Period		4 Enter your business name (individual name if sole proprietor).
○ 1st Quarter	○ 3rd Quarter	Enter your address.
○ 2nd Quarter	○ 4th Quarter	Enter your city, state, and ZIP code or your city, foreign country name, foreign province/county, and foreign postal code.

IRS Form 944 – Employer's Annual Federal Tax Return

If you are a small business with only one or two employees, you can use IRS form 944. This form is used if your annual liabilities such as social security, Medicare and federal withholdings are less than $1,000. That means you would only need to file and pay the taxes once a year.

Form **944 for 2017:** Employer's ANNUAL Federal Tax Return

Department of the Treasury — Internal Revenue Service

OMB No. 1545-2007

Employer identification number (EIN)

Name (not your trade name)

Trade name (if any)

Address

Number   Street   Suite or room number

City   State   ZIP code

Foreign country name   Foreign province/county   Foreign postal code

Read the separate instructions before you complete Form 944. Type or print within the boxes.

Part 1: Answer these questions for this year. Employers in American Samoa, Guam, the Commonwealth of the Northern Mariana Islands, the U.S. Virgin Islands, and Puerto Rico can skip lines 1 and 2, unless you have employees who are subject to U.S. income tax withholding.

1   Wages, tips, and other compensation **1**

2   Federal income tax withheld from wages, tips, and other compensation **2**

3   If no wages, tips, and other compensation are subject to social security or Medicare tax   **3** ☐ Check and go to line 5.

4   Taxable social security and Medicare wages and tips:

	Column 1		Column 2
4a Taxable social security wages		× 0.124 =	
4b Taxable social security tips		× 0.124 =	
4c Taxable Medicare wages & tips		× 0.029 =	
4d Taxable wages & tips subject to Additional Medicare Tax withholding		× 0.009 =	

4e   Add Column 2 from lines 4a, 4b, 4c, and 4d **4e**

5   Total taxes before adjustments. Add lines 2 and 4e **5**

6   Current year's adjustments (see instructions) **6**

7   Total taxes after adjustments. Combine lines 5 and 6 . . . . **7**

8   Qualified small business payroll tax credit for increasing research activities. Attach Form 8974 . **8**

9   Total taxes after adjustments and credits. Subtract line 8 from line 7 . . . . **9**

10   Total deposits for this year, including overpayment applied from a prior year and overpayments applied from Form 944-X, 944-X (SP), 941-X, or 941-X (PR) **10**

11   Balance due. If line 9 is more than line 10, enter the difference and see instructions **11**

12   Overpayment. If line 10 is more than line 9, enter the difference   Check one: ☐ Apply to next return. ☐ Send a refund.

▶ You MUST complete both pages of Form 944 and SIGN it.

Next ▶

For Privacy Act and Paperwork Reduction Act Notice, see the back of the Payment Voucher.   Cat. No. 39010N   Form **944** (2017)

Name (not your trade name)	Employer identification number (EIN)

Part 2: Tell us about your deposit schedule and tax liability for this year.

13 Check one: ☐ Line 9 is less than $2,500. Go to Part 3.

☐ Line 9 is $2,500 or more. Enter your tax liability for each month. If you are a semiweekly depositor or you accumulate $100,000 or more of liability on any day during a deposit period, you must complete Form 945-A instead of the boxes below.

	Jan.		Apr.		Jul.		Oct.
13a		13d		13g		13j	

	Feb.		May		Aug.		Nov.
13b		13e		13h		13k	

	Mar.		Jun.		Sep.		Dec.
13c		13f		13i		13l	

Total liability for year. Add lines 13a through 13l. Total must equal line 9. 13m

Part 3: Tell us about your business. If question 14 does NOT apply to your business, leave it blank.

14 If your business has closed or you stopped paying wages...

☐ Check here and enter the final date you paid wages.

Part 4: May we speak with your third-party designee?

Do you want to allow an employee, a paid tax preparer, or another person to discuss this return with the IRS? See the instructions for details.

☐ Yes. Designee's name and phone number

Select a 5-digit Personal Identification Number (PIN) to use when talking to IRS. ☐ ☐ ☐ ☐ ☐

☐ No.

Part 5: Sign Here. You MUST complete both pages of Form 944 and SIGN it.

Under penalties of perjury, I declare that I have examined this return, including accompanying schedules and statements, and to the best of my knowledge and belief, it is true, correct, and complete. Declaration of preparer (other than taxpayer) is based on all information of which preparer has any knowledge.

X **Sign your name here**

Print your name here

Print your title here

Date

Best daytime phone

Paid Preparer Use Only

Check if you are self-employed ☐

Preparer's name		PTIN	
Preparer's signature		Date	
Firm's name (or yours if self-employed)		EIN	
Address		Phone	
City		State	ZIP code

Form **944** (2017)

Form 944-V,
Payment Voucher

Purpose of Form

Complete Form 944-V if you're making a payment with Form 944. We will use the completed voucher to credit your payment more promptly and accurately, and to improve our service to you.

Making Payments With Form 944

To avoid a penalty, make your payment with your 2017 Form 944 **only if** one of the following applies.

• Your net taxes for the year (Form 944, line 9) are less than $2,500 and you are paying in full with a timely filed return.

• You already deposited the taxes you owed for the first, second, and third quarters of 2017, and the tax you owe for the fourth quarter of 2017 is less than $2,500, and you're paying, in full, the tax you owe for the fourth quarter of 2017 with a timely filed return.

• Your net taxes for the third quarter are $2,500 or more, net taxes for the fourth quarter are less than $2,500, and you didn't incur a $100,000 next-day deposit obligation during the fourth quarter.

• You're a monthly schedule depositor making a payment in accordance with the Accuracy of Deposits Rule. See section 11 of Pub. 15, section 8 of Pub. 80, or section 11 of Pub. 179 for details. In this case, the amount of your payment may be $2,500 or more.

Otherwise, you must make deposits by electronic funds transfer. See section 11 of Pub. 15, section 8 of Pub. 80, or section 11 of Pub. 179 for deposit instructions. Don't use Form 944-V to make federal tax deposits.

 Use Form 944-V when making any payment with Form 944. However, if you pay an amount with Form 944 that should've been deposited, you may be subject to a penalty. See section 11 of Pub. 15, section 8 of Pub. 80, or section 11 of Pub. 179 for details.

Specific Instructions

Box 1—Employer identification number (EIN). If you don't have an EIN, you may apply for one online by visiting the IRS website at www.irs.gov/EIN. You may also apply for an EIN by faxing or mailing Form SS-4 to the IRS. If you haven't received your EIN by the due date of Form 944, write "Applied For" and the date you applied in this entry space.

Box 2—Amount paid. Enter the amount paid with Form 944.

Box 3—Name and address. Enter your name and address as shown on Form 944.

• Enclose your check or money order made payable to "United States Treasury" and write your EIN, "Form 944," and "2017" on your check or money order. Don't send cash. Don't staple Form 944-V or your payment to Form 944 (or to each other).

• Detach Form 944-V and send it with your payment and Form 944 to the address provided in the Instructions for Form 944.

Note: You must also complete the entity information above Part 1 on Form 944.

Detach Here and Mail With Your Payment and Form 944.

✂ -- ✂

Form **944-V**	Payment Voucher	OMB No. 1545-2007
Department of the Treasury Internal Revenue Service	▶ Don't staple this voucher or your payment to Form 944.	**2017**

1 Enter your employer identification number (EIN).	2 **Enter the amount of your payment.** ▶ Make your check or money order payable to "United States Treasury"	Dollars	Cents
	3 Enter your business name (individual name if sole proprietor).		
	Enter your address.		
	Enter your city, state, and ZIP code or your city, foreign country name, foreign province/county, and foreign postal code.		

IRS Form 1040 (Schedule A) – Itemized Deductions

When you choose to itemize your deductions, then you use the schedule A. This form has many categories for itemization such as medical and dental expenses, taxes, interest, gifts to charity, job expenses and miscellaneous expenses.

SCHEDULE A
(Form 1040)

Department of the Treasury
Internal Revenue Service (99)

Itemized Deductions

▶ Go to www.irs.gov/ScheduleA for instructions and the latest information.
▶ Attach to Form 1040.

Caution: If you are claiming a net qualified disaster loss on Form 4684, see the instructions for line 28.

OMB No. 1545-0074

2017

Attachment
Sequence No. **07**

Name(s) shown on Form 1040

Your social security number

Medical and Dental Expenses		Caution: Do not include expenses reimbursed or paid by others.		
	1	Medical and dental expenses (see instructions)	1	
	2	Enter amount from Form 1040, line 38 | 2 |		
	3	Multiply line 2 by 7.5% (0.075)	3	
	4	Subtract line 3 from line 1. If line 3 is more than line 1, enter -0-		4
Taxes You Paid	5	State and local (**check only one box**):		
		a ☐ Income taxes, **or**	5	
		b ☐ General sales taxes		
	6	Real estate taxes (see instructions)	6	
	7	Personal property taxes	7	
	8	Other taxes. List type and amount ▶		
			8	
	9	Add lines 5 through 8		9
Interest You Paid Note: Your mortgage interest deduction may be limited (see instructions).	10	Home mortgage interest and points reported to you on Form 1098	10	
	11	Home mortgage interest not reported to you on Form 1098. If paid to the person from whom you bought the home, see instructions and show that person's name, identifying no., and address ▶		
			11	
	12	Points not reported to you on Form 1098. See instructions for special rules	12	
	13	Reserved for future use	13	
	14	Investment interest. Attach Form 4952 if required. See instructions	14	
	15	Add lines 10 through 14		15
Gifts to Charity If you made a gift and got a benefit for it, see instructions.	16	Gifts by cash or check. If you made any gift of $250 or more, see instructions	16	
	17	Other than by cash or check. If any gift of $250 or more, see instructions. You **must** attach Form 8283 if over $500	17	
	18	Carryover from prior year	18	
	19	Add lines 16 through 18		19
Casualty and Theft Losses	20	Casualty or theft loss(es) other than net qualified disaster losses. Attach Form 4684 and enter the amount from line 18 of that form. See instructions		20
Job Expenses and Certain Miscellaneous Deductions	21	Unreimbursed employee expenses—job travel, union dues, job education, etc. Attach Form 2106 or 2106-EZ if required. See instructions. ▶	21	
	22	Tax preparation fees	22	
	23	Other expenses—investment, safe deposit box, etc. List type and amount ▶		
			23	
	24	Add lines 21 through 23	24	
	25	Enter amount from Form 1040, line 38 | 25 |		
	26	Multiply line 25 by 2% (0.02)	26	
	27	Subtract line 26 from line 24. If line 26 is more than line 24, enter -0-		27
Other Miscellaneous Deductions	28	Other—from list in instructions. List type and amount ▶		
				28
Total Itemized Deductions	29	Is Form 1040, line 38, over $156,900?		
		☐ **No.** Your deduction is not limited. Add the amounts in the far right column for lines 4 through 28. Also, enter this amount on Form 1040, line 40. ⎫		29
		☐ **Yes.** Your deduction may be limited. See the Itemized Deductions Worksheet in the instructions to figure the amount to enter. ⎬		
	30	If you elect to itemize deductions even though they are less than your standard deduction, check here ▶ ☐		

For Paperwork Reduction Act Notice, see the Instructions for Form 1040.   Cat. No. 17145C   Schedule A (Form 1040) 2017

IRS Form 1040 (Schedule C) – Profit or Loss from Business

With a schedule C you will report any income or losses the business takes from normal operations as a sole proprietor.

SCHEDULE C
(Form 1040)

Department of the Treasury
Internal Revenue Service (99)

Profit or Loss From Business
(Sole Proprietorship)

▶ Go to www.irs.gov/ScheduleC for instructions and the latest information.
▶ Attach to Form 1040, 1040NR, or 1041; partnerships generally must file Form 1065.

OMB No. 1545-0074

2017

Attachment
Sequence No. **09**

Name of proprietor

Social security number (SSN)

A Principal business or profession, including product or service (see instructions)

B Enter code from instructions
▶

C Business name. If no separate business name, leave blank.

D Employer ID number (EIN) (see instr.)

E Business address (including suite or room no.) ▶
City, town or post office, state, and ZIP code

F Accounting method: **(1)** ☐ Cash   **(2)** ☐ Accrual   **(3)** ☐ Other (specify) ▶

G Did you "materially participate" in the operation of this business during 2017? If "No," see instructions for limit on losses . . ☐ Yes ☐ No

H If you started or acquired this business during 2017, check here . . . . ▶ ☐

I Did you make any payments in 2017 that would require you to file Form(s) 1099? (see instructions) . . . . . . ☐ Yes ☐ No

J If "Yes," did you or will you file required Forms 1099? . . . . ☐ Yes ☐ No

Part I Income

1	Gross receipts or sales. See instructions for line 1 and check the box if this income was reported to you on Form W-2 and the "Statutory employee" box on that form was checked . . . . ▶ ☐	**1**	
2	Returns and allowances	**2**	
3	Subtract line 2 from line 1	**3**	
4	Cost of goods sold (from line 42)	**4**	
5	**Gross profit.** Subtract line 4 from line 3	**5**	
6	Other income, including federal and state gasoline or fuel tax credit or refund (see instructions) . .	**6**	
7	**Gross income.** Add lines 5 and 6 . . . . ▶	**7**	

Part II Expenses. Enter expenses for business use of your home **only** on line 30.

8	Advertising	**8**		**18**	Office expense (see instructions)	**18**
9	Car and truck expenses (see instructions)	**9**		**19**	Pension and profit-sharing plans .	**19**
10	Commissions and fees .	**10**		**20**	Rent or lease (see instructions):	
11	Contract labor (see instructions)	**11**		**a**	Vehicles, machinery, and equipment	**20a**
12	Depletion	**12**		**b**	Other business property . . .	**20b**
13	Depreciation and section 179 expense deduction (not included in Part III) (see instructions)	**13**		**21**	Repairs and maintenance . . .	**21**
				22	Supplies (not included in Part III) .	**22**
				23	Taxes and licenses	**23**
14	Employee benefit programs (other than on line 19) . .	**14**		**24**	Travel, meals, and entertainment:	
15	Insurance (other than health)	**15**		**a**	Travel	**24a**
16	Interest:			**b**	Deductible meals and entertainment (see instructions) .	**24b**
a	Mortgage (paid to banks, etc.)	**16a**		**25**	Utilities	**25**
b	Other	**16b**		**26**	Wages (less employment credits) .	**26**
17	Legal and professional services	**17**		**27a**	Other expenses (from line 48) .	**27a**
				b	**Reserved for future use** . . .	**27b**
28	**Total expenses** before expenses for business use of home. Add lines 8 through 27a . . . . . ▶					**28**
29	Tentative profit or (loss). Subtract line 28 from line 7					**29**

30 Expenses for business use of your home. Do not report these expenses elsewhere. Attach Form 8829 unless using the simplified method (see instructions).
Simplified method filers only: enter the total square footage of: (a) your home: _____ and (b) the part of your home used for business: _____. Use the Simplified Method Worksheet in the instructions to figure the amount to enter on line 30 . . . . | **30** |

31 Net profit or **(loss).** Subtract line 30 from line 29.
• If a profit, enter on both **Form 1040, line 12** (or **Form 1040NR, line 13**) and on **Schedule SE, line 2.** (If you checked the box on line 1, see instructions). Estates and trusts, enter on **Form 1041, line 3.**
• If a loss, you **must** go to line 32. | **31** |

32 If you have a loss, check the box that describes your investment in this activity (see instructions).
• If you checked 32a, enter the loss on both **Form 1040, line 12,** (or **Form 1040NR, line 13**) and on **Schedule SE, line 2.** (If you checked the box on line 1, see the line 31 instructions). Estates and trusts, enter on **Form 1041, line 3.**
• If you checked 32b, you **must** attach **Form 6198.** Your loss may be limited.

32a ☐ All investment is at risk.
32b ☐ Some investment is not at risk.

For Paperwork Reduction Act Notice, see the separate instructions.   Cat. No. 11334P   Schedule C (Form 1040) 2017

Part III   Cost of Goods Sold (see instructions)

33   Method(s) used to
      value closing inventory: a ☐ Cost   b ☐ Lower of cost or market   c ☐ Other (attach explanation)

34   Was there any change in determining quantities, costs, or valuations between opening and closing inventory?
      If "Yes," attach explanation . . . . ☐ Yes   ☐ No

35 Inventory at beginning of year. If different from last year's closing inventory, attach explanation	35	
36 Purchases less cost of items withdrawn for personal use	36	
37 Cost of labor. Do not include any amounts paid to yourself	37	
38 Materials and supplies	38	
39 Other costs	39	
40 Add lines 35 through 39	40	
41 Inventory at end of year	41	
42 **Cost of goods sold.** Subtract line 41 from line 40. Enter the result here and on line 4	42	

Part IV   Information on Your Vehicle. Complete this part **only** if you are claiming car or truck expenses on line 9 and are not required to file Form 4562 for this business. See the instructions for line 13 to find out if you must file Form 4562.

43   When did you place your vehicle in service for business purposes? (month, day, year) ▶   /   /

44   Of the total number of miles you drove your vehicle during 2017, enter the number of miles you used your vehicle for:

a Business   b Commuting (see instructions)   c Other

45   Was your vehicle available for personal use during off-duty hours? . . . . ☐ Yes   ☐ No

46   Do you (or your spouse) have another vehicle available for personal use? . . . . ☐ Yes   ☐ No

47a   Do you have evidence to support your deduction? . . . . ☐ Yes   ☐ No

b   If "Yes," is the evidence written? . . . . ☐ Yes   ☐ No

Part V   Other Expenses. List below business expenses not included on lines 8–26 or line 30.

48 **Total other expenses.** Enter here and on line 27a	48	

IRS Form 1040 (Schedule C-EZ) – Net Profit from Business

As a schedule C is for reporting your income or losses, the schedule C-EZ reports your income and expenses related solely to self-employment activities. Keep in mind, you still need to report the profits and losses on IRS form 1040.

Net Profit From Business
(Sole Proprietorship)

▶ Partnerships, joint ventures, etc., generally must file Form 1065 or 1065-B.
▶ Attach to Form 1040, 1040NR, or 1041. ▶ See Instructions on page 2.

OMB No. 1545-0074

2017

Attachment
Sequence No. **09A**

Name of proprietor | Social security number (SSN)

Part I General Information

You May Use Schedule C-EZ Instead of Schedule C Only If You:
- Had business expenses of $5,000 or less,
- Use the cash method of accounting,
- Did not have an inventory at any time during the year,
- Did not have a net loss from your business,
- Had only one business as either a sole proprietor, qualified joint venture, or statutory employee,

And You:
- Had no employees during the year,
- Do not deduct expenses for business use of your home,
- Do not have prior year unallowed passive activity losses from this business, and
- Are not required to file **Form 4562**, Depreciation and Amortization, for this business. See the instructions for Schedule C, line 13, to find out if you must file.

A Principal business or profession, including product or service

B Enter business code (see page 2)
▶

C Business name. If no separate business name, leave blank.

D Enter your EIN (see page 2)

E Business address (including suite or room no.). Address not required if same as on page 1 of your tax return.

City, town or post office, state, and ZIP code

F Did you make any payments in 2017 that would require you to file Form(s) 1099? (see the Instructions for Schedule C) . . . . ☐ Yes ☐ No

G If "Yes," did you or will you file required Forms 1099? . . . . ☐ Yes ☐ No

Part II Figure Your Net Profit

1 **Gross receipts. Caution:** If this income was reported to you on Form W-2 and the "Statutory employee" box on that form was checked, see *Statutory employees* in the instructions for Schedule C, line 1, and check here . . . . ▶ ☐ | **1** |

2 **Total expenses** (see page 2). If more than $5,000, you **must** use Schedule C . . . . . . | **2** |

3 **Net profit.** Subtract line 2 from line 1. If less than zero, you **must** use Schedule C. Enter on both **Form 1040, line 12,** and **Schedule SE, line 2,** or on **Form 1040NR, line 13,** and **Schedule SE, line 2** (see page 2). (Statutory employees **do not** report this amount on Schedule SE, line 2.) Estates and trusts, enter on **Form 1041, line 3** . . . . | **3** |

Part III Information on Your Vehicle. Complete this part **only** if you are claiming car or truck expenses on line 2.

4 When did you place your vehicle in service for business purposes? (month, day, year) ▶

5 Of the total number of miles you drove your vehicle during 2017, enter the number of miles you used your vehicle for:

a Business _____ b Commuting (see page 2) _____ c Other _____

6 Was your vehicle available for personal use during off-duty hours? . . . . ☐ Yes ☐ No

7 Do you (or your spouse) have another vehicle available for personal use? . . . . ☐ Yes ☐ No

8a Do you have evidence to support your deduction? . . . . ☐ Yes ☐ No

b If "Yes," is the evidence written? . . . . ☐ Yes ☐ No

For Paperwork Reduction Act Notice, see the separate instructions for Schedule C (Form 1040). Cat. No. 14374D Schedule C-EZ (Form 1040) 2017

Instructions

Future developments. For the latest information about developments related to Schedule C-EZ (Form 1040) and its instructions, such as legislation enacted after they were published, go to www.irs.gov/ScheduleCEZ.

 Before you begin, see General Instructions in the 2017 Instructions for Schedule C.

You can use Schedule C-EZ instead of Schedule C if:

• You operated a business or practiced a profession as a sole proprietorship or qualified joint venture, or you were a statutory employee, and

• You have met all the requirements listed in Schedule C-EZ, Part I.

For more information on electing to be taxed as a qualified joint venture (including the possible social security benefits of this election), see Qualified Joint Venture in the Instructions for Schedule C. You can also go to IRS.gov and enter "qualified joint venture" in the search box.

Line A

Describe the business or professional activity that provided your principal source of income reported on line 1. Give the general field or activity and the type of product or service.

Line B

Enter the six-digit code that identifies your principal business or professional activity. See the Instructions for Schedule C for the list of codes.

Line D

Enter on line D the employer identification number (EIN) that was issued to you and in your name as a sole proprietor. If you are filing Form 1041, enter the EIN issued to the estate or trust. Do not enter your SSN. Do not enter another taxpayer's EIN (for example, from any Forms 1099-MISC that you received). **If you do not have an EIN, leave line D blank.**

You need an EIN only if you have a qualified retirement plan or are required to file an employment, excise, alcohol, tobacco, or firearms tax return, are a payer of gambling winnings, or are filing Form 1041 for an estate or trust. If you need an EIN, see the Instructions for Form SS-4.

Single-member LLCs. If you are the sole owner of an LLC that is not treated as a separate entity for federal income tax purposes, enter on line D the EIN that was issued to the LLC (in the LLC's legal name) for a qualified retirement plan, to file employment, excise, alcohol, tobacco, or firearms returns, or as a payer of gambling winnings. **If you do not have such an EIN, leave line D blank.**

Line E

Enter your business address. Show a street address instead of a box number. Include the suite or room number, if any.

Line F

See the instructions for Schedule C, line I, to help determine if you are required to file any Forms 1099.

Line 1

Enter gross receipts from your trade or business. Include amounts you received in your trade or business that were properly shown on Form 1099-MISC. If the total amounts that were reported in box 7 of Forms 1099-MISC are more than the total you are reporting on line 1, attach a statement explaining the difference. You must show all items of taxable income actually or constructively received during the year (in cash, property, or services). Income is constructively received when it is credited to your account or set aside for you to use. Don't offset this amount by any losses.

Line 2

Enter the total amount of all deductible business expenses you actually paid during the year. Examples of these expenses include advertising, car and truck expenses, commissions and fees, insurance, interest, legal and professional services, office expenses, rent or lease expenses, repairs and maintenance, supplies, taxes, travel, the allowable percentage of business meals and entertainment, and utilities (including telephone). For details, see the instructions for Schedule C, Parts II and V. You can use the optional worksheet below to record your expenses. Enter on lines b through f the type and amount of expenses not included on line a.

If you claim car or truck expenses, be sure to complete Schedule C-EZ, Part III.

Line 3

Nonresident aliens using Form 1040NR should also enter the total on Schedule SE, line 2, if you are covered under the U.S. social security system due to an international social security agreement currently in effect. See the Instructions for Schedule SE for information on international social security agreements.

Line 5b

Generally, commuting is travel between your home and a work location. If you converted your vehicle during the year from personal to business use (or vice versa), enter your commuting miles only for the period you drove your vehicle for business. For information on certain travel that is considered a business expense rather than commuting, see the Instructions for Form 2106.

Optional Worksheet for Line 2 (keep a copy for your records)

a Deductible meals and entertainment (see the instructions for Schedule C, line 24b)	a	
b _____	b	
c _____	c	
d _____	d	
e _____	e	
f _____	f	
g **Total.** Add lines a through f. Enter here and on line 2	g	

IRS Form 1040 (Schedule D) – Capital Gains and Losses

The schedule D will be used to report net capital gains and losses. These gains will include involuntary conversions of capital assets that are not held for the business or profit. This excludes casualty and theft.

SCHEDULE D (Form 1040)	Capital Gains and Losses	OMB No. 1545-0074

Capital Gains and Losses

Department of the Treasury
Internal Revenue Service (99)

► Attach to Form 1040 or Form 1040NR.
► Go to www.irs.gov/ScheduleD for instructions and the latest information.
► Use Form 8949 to list your transactions for lines 1b, 2, 3, 8b, 9, and 10.

2017

Attachment
Sequence No. **12**

Name(s) shown on return | Your social security number

Part I — Short-Term Capital Gains and Losses—Assets Held One Year or Less

See instructions for how to figure the amounts to enter on the lines below. This form may be easier to complete if you round off cents to whole dollars.	(d) Proceeds (sales price)	(e) Cost (or other basis)	(g) Adjustments to gain or loss from Form(s) 8949, Part I, line 2, column (g)	(h) Gain or (loss) Subtract column (e) from column (d) and combine the result with column (g)
1a Totals for all short-term transactions reported on Form 1099-B for which basis was reported to the IRS and for which you have no adjustments (see instructions). However, if you choose to report all these transactions on Form 8949, leave this line blank and go to line 1b .				
1b Totals for all transactions reported on Form(s) 8949 with **Box A** checked				
2 Totals for all transactions reported on Form(s) 8949 with **Box B** checked				
3 Totals for all transactions reported on Form(s) 8949 with **Box C** checked				

4 Short-term gain from Form 6252 and short-term gain or (loss) from Forms 4684, 6781, and 8824 .	**4**	
5 Net short-term gain or (loss) from partnerships, S corporations, estates, and trusts from Schedule(s) K-1	**5**	
6 Short-term capital loss carryover. Enter the amount, if any, from line 8 of your **Capital Loss Carryover Worksheet** in the instructions	**6**	( )
7 **Net short-term capital gain or (loss).** Combine lines 1a through 6 in column (h). If you have any long-term capital gains or losses, go to Part II below. Otherwise, go to Part III on the back	**7**	

Part II — Long-Term Capital Gains and Losses—Assets Held More Than One Year

See instructions for how to figure the amounts to enter on the lines below. This form may be easier to complete if you round off cents to whole dollars.	(d) Proceeds (sales price)	(e) Cost (or other basis)	(g) Adjustments to gain or loss from Form(s) 8949, Part II, line 2, column (g)	(h) Gain or (loss) Subtract column (e) from column (d) and combine the result with column (g)
8a Totals for all long-term transactions reported on Form 1099-B for which basis was reported to the IRS and for which you have no adjustments (see instructions). However, if you choose to report all these transactions on Form 8949, leave this line blank and go to line 8b .				
8b Totals for all transactions reported on Form(s) 8949 with **Box D** checked				
9 Totals for all transactions reported on Form(s) 8949 with **Box E** checked				
10 Totals for all transactions reported on Form(s) 8949 with **Box F** checked				

11 Gain from Form 4797, Part I; long-term gain from Forms 2439 and 6252; and long-term gain or (loss) from Forms 4684, 6781, and 8824	**11**	
12 Net long-term gain or (loss) from partnerships, S corporations, estates, and trusts from Schedule(s) K-1	**12**	
13 Capital gain distributions. See the instructions	**13**	
14 Long-term capital loss carryover. Enter the amount, if any, from line 13 of your **Capital Loss Carryover Worksheet** in the instructions	**14**	( )
15 **Net long-term capital gain or (loss).** Combine lines 8a through 14 in column (h). Then go to Part III on the back	**15**	

For Paperwork Reduction Act Notice, see your tax return instructions.   Cat. No. 11338H   Schedule D (Form 1040) 2017

Part III Summary

16   Combine lines 7 and 15 and enter the result **16**

- If line 16 is a **gain,** enter the amount from line 16 on Form 1040, line 13, or Form 1040NR, line 14. Then go to line 17 below.
- If line 16 is a **loss,** skip lines 17 through 20 below. Then go to line 21. Also be sure to complete line 22.
- If line 16 is **zero,** skip lines 17 through 21 below and enter -0- on Form 1040, line 13, or Form 1040NR, line 14. Then go to line 22.

17   Are lines 15 and 16 **both** gains?
☐ **Yes.** Go to line 18.
☐ **No.** Skip lines 18 through 21, and go to line 22.

18   If you are required to complete the **28% Rate Gain Worksheet** (see instructions), enter the amount, if any, from line 7 of that worksheet . . . . ▶   **18**

19   If you are required to complete the **Unrecaptured Section 1250 Gain Worksheet** (see instructions), enter the amount, if any, from line 18 of that worksheet . . . . ▶   **19**

20   Are lines 18 and 19 **both** zero or blank?
☐ **Yes.** Complete the **Qualified Dividends and Capital Gain Tax Worksheet** in the instructions for Form 1040, line 44 (or in the instructions for Form 1040NR, line 42). **Don't** complete lines 21 and 22 below.

☐ **No.** Complete the **Schedule D Tax Worksheet** in the instructions. **Don't** complete lines 21 and 22 below.

21   If line 16 is a loss, enter here and on Form 1040, line 13, or Form 1040NR, line 14, the **smaller** of:

- The loss on line 16 or
- ($3,000), or if married filing separately, ($1,500)   } **21**

Note: When figuring which amount is smaller, treat both amounts as positive numbers.

22   Do you have qualified dividends on Form 1040, line 9b, or Form 1040NR, line 10b?

☐ **Yes.** Complete the **Qualified Dividends and Capital Gain Tax Worksheet** in the instructions for Form 1040, line 44 (or in the instructions for Form 1040NR, line 42).

☐ **No.** Complete the rest of Form 1040 or Form 1040NR.

IRS Form 1040 (Schedule E) – Supplemental Income and Loss

With a schedule E you will report your income or losses from rental real estate, royalties, partnerships, S corporations, estates, and trusts. You may include your own schedules for any of these items as long as you follow the same format at the schedule E.

SCHEDULE E
(Form 1040)

Department of the Treasury
Internal Revenue Service (99)

Supplemental Income and Loss

(From rental real estate, royalties, partnerships, S corporations, estates, trusts, REMICs, etc.)

▶ Attach to Form 1040, 1040NR, or Form 1041.

▶ Go to *www.irs.gov/ScheduleE* for instructions and the latest information.

OMB No. 1545-0074

2017

Attachment
Sequence No. **13**

Name(s) shown on return

Your social security number

Part I Income or Loss From Rental Real Estate and Royalties Note: If you are in the business of renting personal property, use Schedule C or C-EZ (see instructions). If you are an individual, report farm rental income or loss from Form 4835 on page 2, line 40.

A Did you make any payments in 2017 that would require you to file Form(s) 1099? (see instructions) . . . . . ☐ Yes ☐ No
B If "Yes," did you or will you file required Forms 1099? . . . . ☐ Yes ☐ No

1a Physical address of each property (street, city, state, ZIP code)

A	
B	
C	

1b	Type of Property (from list below)	2 For each rental real estate property listed above, report the number of fair rental and personal use days. Check the QJV box only if you meet the requirements to file as a qualified joint venture. See instructions.		Fair Rental Days	Personal Use Days	QJV
A			A			☐
B			B			☐
C			C			☐

Type of Property:

1 Single Family Residence 3 Vacation/Short-Term Rental 5 Land 7 Self-Rental
2 Multi-Family Residence 4 Commercial 6 Royalties 8 Other (describe)

Income:	Properties:	A	B	C
3 Rents received	3			
4 Royalties received	4			
Expenses:				
5 Advertising	5			
6 Auto and travel (see instructions)	6			
7 Cleaning and maintenance	7			
8 Commissions	8			
9 Insurance	9			
10 Legal and other professional fees	10			
11 Management fees	11			
12 Mortgage interest paid to banks, etc. (see instructions)	12			
13 Other interest	13			
14 Repairs	14			
15 Supplies	15			
16 Taxes	16			
17 Utilities	17			
18 Depreciation expense or depletion	18			
19 Other (list) ▶	19			
20 Total expenses. Add lines 5 through 19	20			
21 Subtract line 20 from line 3 (rents) and/or 4 (royalties). If result is a (loss), see instructions to find out if you must file **Form 6198**	21			
22 Deductible rental real estate loss after limitation, if any, on **Form 8582** (see instructions)	22	( )	( )	( )

23a	Total of all amounts reported on line 3 for all rental properties	23a		
b	Total of all amounts reported on line 4 for all royalty properties	23b		
c	Total of all amounts reported on line 12 for all properties	23c		
d	Total of all amounts reported on line 18 for all properties	23d		
e	Total of all amounts reported on line 20 for all properties	23e		

24	**Income.** Add positive amounts shown on line 21. **Do not** include any losses	24	
25	**Losses.** Add royalty losses from line 21 and rental real estate losses from line 22. Enter total losses here .	25	( )
26	**Total rental real estate and royalty income or (loss).** Combine lines 24 and 25. Enter the result here. If Parts II, III, IV, and line 40 on page 2 do not apply to you, also enter this amount on Form 1040, line 17, or Form 1040NR, line 18. Otherwise, include this amount in the total on line 41 on page 2 . . .	26	

For Paperwork Reduction Act Notice, see the separate instructions. Cat. No. 11344L Schedule E (Form 1040) 2017

Name(s) shown on return. Do not enter name and social security number if shown on other side.   Your social security number

Caution: The IRS compares amounts reported on your tax return with amounts shown on Schedule(s) K-1.

Part II   **Income or Loss From Partnerships and S Corporations**   **Note:** If you report a loss from an at-risk activity for which any amount is **not** at risk, you **must** check the box in column (e) on line 28 and attach **Form 6198.** See instructions.

27   Are you reporting any loss not allowed in a prior year due to the at-risk, excess farm loss, or basis limitations, a prior year unallowed loss from a passive activity (if that loss was not reported on Form 8582), or unreimbursed partnership expenses? If you answered "Yes," see instructions before completing this section. . . . . ☐ **Yes** ☐ **No**

28	(a) Name	(b) Enter P for partnership; S for S corporation	(c) Check if foreign partnership	(d) Employer identification number	(e) Check if any amount is not at risk
A			☐		☐
B			☐		☐
C			☐		☐
D			☐		☐

	Passive Income and Loss		Nonpassive Income and Loss		
	(f) Passive loss allowed (attach Form 8582 if required)	(g) Passive income from Schedule K-1	(h) Nonpassive loss from Schedule K-1	(i) Section 179 expense deduction from Form 4562	(j) Nonpassive income from Schedule K-1
A					
B					
C					
D					

29a	Totals				
b	Totals				

30	Add columns (g) and (j) of line 29a	30	
31	Add columns (f), (h), and (i) of line 29b	31	( )
32	**Total partnership and S corporation income or (loss).** Combine lines 30 and 31. Enter the result here and include in the total on line 41 below	32	

Part III   **Income or Loss From Estates and Trusts**

33	(a) Name	(b) Employer identification number
A		
B		

	Passive Income and Loss		Nonpassive Income and Loss	
	(c) Passive deduction or loss allowed (attach Form 8582 if required)	(d) Passive income from Schedule K-1	(e) Deduction or loss from Schedule K-1	(f) Other income from Schedule K-1
A				
B				

34a	Totals			
b	Totals			

35	Add columns (d) and (f) of line 34a	35	
36	Add columns (c) and (e) of line 34b	36	( )
37	**Total estate and trust income or (loss).** Combine lines 35 and 36. Enter the result here and include in the total on line 41 below	37	

Part IV   **Income or Loss From Real Estate Mortgage Investment Conduits (REMICs)—Residual Holder**

38	(a) Name	(b) Employer identification number	(c) Excess inclusion from Schedules Q, line 2c (see instructions)	(d) Taxable income (net loss) from Schedules Q, line 1b	(e) Income from Schedules Q, line 3b

39	Combine columns (d) and (e) only. Enter the result here and include in the total on line 41 below	39	

Part V   **Summary**

40	Net farm rental income or (loss) from **Form 4835.** Also, complete line 42 below	40	
41	**Total income or (loss).** Combine lines 26, 32, 37, 39, and 40. Enter the result here and on Form 1040, line 17, or Form 1040NR, line 18 ▶	41	
42	**Reconciliation of farming and fishing income.** Enter your gross farming and fishing income reported on Form 4835, line 7; Schedule K-1 (Form 1065), box 14, code B; Schedule K-1 (Form 1120S), box 17, code V; and Schedule K-1 (Form 1041), box 14, code F (see instructions) . .	42	
43	**Reconciliation for real estate professionals.** If you were a real estate professional (see instructions), enter the net income or (loss) you reported anywhere on Form 1040 or Form 1040NR from all rental real estate activities in which you materially participated under the passive activity loss rules . .	43	

Schedule E (Form 1040) 2017

IRS Form 1065 – U.S. Return of Partnership Income

Form 1065 will be used in a partnership to report income, gains, losses, deductions, credits, etc.

Form 1065

U.S. Return of Partnership Income

Department of the Treasury
Internal Revenue Service

For calendar year 2017, or tax year beginning _____, 2017, ending _____, 20 ____.

▶ Go to www.irs.gov/Form1065 for instructions and the latest information.

OMB No. 1545-0123

2017

A Principal business activity	Name of partnership	D Employer identification number
B Principal product or service	**Type or Print** — Number, street, and room or suite no. If a P.O. box, see the instructions.	E Date business started
C Business code number	City or town, state or province, country, and ZIP or foreign postal code	F Total assets (see the instructions) $

G Check applicable boxes: (1) ☐ Initial return (2) ☐ Final return (3) ☐ Name change (4) ☐ Address change (5) ☐ Amended return
(6) ☐ Technical termination - also check (1) or (2)

H Check accounting method: (1) ☐ Cash (2) ☐ Accrual (3) ☐ Other (specify) ▶ _____

I Number of Schedules K-1. Attach one for each person who was a partner at any time during the tax year ▶

J Check if Schedules C and M-3 are attached . . . . ☐

Caution. Include only trade or business income and expenses on lines 1a through 22 below. See the instructions for more information.

Income

1a	Gross receipts or sales	1a	
b	Returns and allowances	1b	
c	Balance. Subtract line 1b from line 1a	1c	
2	Cost of goods sold (attach Form 1125-A)	2	
3	Gross profit. Subtract line 2 from line 1c	3	
4	Ordinary income (loss) from other partnerships, estates, and trusts (attach statement) . .	4	
5	Net farm profit (loss) (attach Schedule F (Form 1040))	5	
6	Net gain (loss) from Form 4797, Part II, line 17 (attach Form 4797)	6	
7	Other income (loss) (attach statement)	7	
8	**Total income (loss).** Combine lines 3 through 7	8	

Deductions (see the instructions for limitations)

9	Salaries and wages (other than to partners) (less employment credits)	9	
10	Guaranteed payments to partners	10	
11	Repairs and maintenance	11	
12	Bad debts	12	
13	Rent	13	
14	Taxes and licenses	14	
15	Interest	15	
16a	Depreciation (if required, attach Form 4562)	16a	
b	Less depreciation reported on Form 1125-A and elsewhere on return	16b	16c
17	Depletion **(Do not deduct oil and gas depletion.)**	17	
18	Retirement plans, etc.	18	
19	Employee benefit programs	19	
20	Other deductions (attach statement)	20	
21	**Total deductions.** Add the amounts shown in the far right column for lines 9 through 20 .	21	
22	**Ordinary business income (loss).** Subtract line 21 from line 8	22	

Sign Here

Under penalties of perjury, I declare that I have examined this return, including accompanying schedules and statements, and to the best of my knowledge and belief, it is true, correct, and complete. Declaration of preparer (other than partner or limited liability company member) is based on all information of which preparer has any knowledge.

▶ _____ Signature of partner or limited liability company member

▶ _____ Date

May the IRS discuss this return with the preparer shown below (see instructions)? ☐ Yes ☐ No

Paid Preparer Use Only

Print/Type preparer's name	Preparer's signature	Date	Check ☐ if self-employed	PTIN
			Firm's EIN ▶	
Firm's name ▶				
Firm's address ▶			Phone no.	

For Paperwork Reduction Act Notice, see separate instructions.

Cat. No. 11390Z

Form **1065** (2017)

Schedule B	**Other Information**

		Yes	No
1	What type of entity is filing this return? Check the applicable box:		

   a ☐ Domestic general partnership   b ☐ Domestic limited partnership

   c ☐ Domestic limited liability company   d ☐ Domestic limited liability partnership

   e ☐ Foreign partnership   f ☐ Other ▶

		Yes	No
2	At any time during the tax year, was any partner in the partnership a disregarded entity, a partnership (including an entity treated as a partnership), a trust, an S corporation, an estate (other than an estate of a deceased partner), or a nominee or similar person?		
3	At the end of the tax year:		
a	Did any foreign or domestic corporation, partnership (including any entity treated as a partnership), trust, or tax-exempt organization, or any foreign government own, directly or indirectly, an interest of 50% or more in the profit, loss, or capital of the partnership? For rules of constructive ownership, see instructions. If "Yes," attach Schedule B-1, Information on Partners Owning 50% or More of the Partnership		
b	Did any individual or estate own, directly or indirectly, an interest of 50% or more in the profit, loss, or capital of the partnership? For rules of constructive ownership, see instructions. If "Yes," attach Schedule B-1, Information on Partners Owning 50% or More of the Partnership		
4	At the end of the tax year, did the partnership:		
a	Own directly 20% or more, or own, directly or indirectly, 50% or more of the total voting power of all classes of stock entitled to vote of any foreign or domestic corporation? For rules of constructive ownership, see instructions. If "Yes," complete (i) through (iv) below		

(i) Name of Corporation	(ii) Employer Identification Number (if any)	(iii) Country of Incorporation	(iv) Percentage Owned in Voting Stock

b Own directly an interest of 20% or more, or own, directly or indirectly, an interest of 50% or more in the profit, loss, or capital in any foreign or domestic partnership (including an entity treated as a partnership) or in the beneficial interest of a trust? For rules of constructive ownership, see instructions. If "Yes," complete (i) through (v) below .

(i) Name of Entity	(ii) Employer Identification Number (if any)	(iii) Type of Entity	(iv) Country of Organization	(v) Maximum Percentage Owned in Profit, Loss, or Capital

		Yes	No
5	Did the partnership file Form 8893, Election of Partnership Level Tax Treatment, or an election statement under section 6231(a)(1)(B)(ii) for partnership-level tax treatment, that is in effect for this tax year? See Form 8893 for more details		
6	Does the partnership satisfy **all four** of the following conditions?		
a	The partnership's total receipts for the tax year were less than $250,000.		
b	The partnership's total assets at the end of the tax year were less than $1 million.		
c	Schedules K-1 are filed with the return and furnished to the partners on or before the due date (including extensions) for the partnership return.		
d	The partnership is not filing and is not required to file Schedule M-3 . . . . If "Yes," the partnership is not required to complete Schedules L, M-1, and M-2; Item F on page 1 of Form 1065; or Item L on Schedule K-1.		
7	Is this partnership a publicly traded partnership as defined in section 469(k)(2)?		
8	During the tax year, did the partnership have any debt that was cancelled, was forgiven, or had the terms modified so as to reduce the principal amount of the debt?		
9	Has this partnership filed, or is it required to file, Form 8918, Material Advisor Disclosure Statement, to provide information on any reportable transaction?		
10	At any time during calendar year 2017, did the partnership have an interest in or a signature or other authority over a financial account in a foreign country (such as a bank account, securities account, or other financial account)? See the instructions for exceptions and filing requirements for FinCEN Form 114, Report of Foreign Bank and Financial Accounts (FBAR). If "Yes," enter the name of the foreign country. ▶		

Schedule B   Other Information *(continued)*

		Yes	No
11	At any time during the tax year, did the partnership receive a distribution from, or was it the grantor of, or transferor to, a foreign trust? If "Yes," the partnership may have to file Form 3520, Annual Return To Report Transactions With Foreign Trusts and Receipt of Certain Foreign Gifts. See instructions		
12a	Is the partnership making, or had it previously made (and not revoked), a section 754 election? See instructions for details regarding a section 754 election.		
b	Did the partnership make for this tax year an optional basis adjustment under section 743(b) or 734(b)? If "Yes," attach a statement showing the computation and allocation of the basis adjustment. See instructions		
c	Is the partnership required to adjust the basis of partnership assets under section 743(b) or 734(b) because of a substantial built-in loss (as defined under section 743(d)) or substantial basis reduction (as defined under section 734(d))? If "Yes," attach a statement showing the computation and allocation of the basis adjustment. See instructions		
13	Check this box if, during the current or prior tax year, the partnership distributed any property received in a like-kind exchange or contributed such property to another entity (other than disregarded entities wholly owned by the partnership throughout the tax year) ▶ ☐		
14	At any time during the tax year, did the partnership distribute to any partner a tenancy-in-common or other undivided interest in partnership property?		
15	If the partnership is required to file Form 8858, Information Return of U.S. Persons With Respect To Foreign Disregarded Entities, enter the number of Forms 8858 attached. See instructions ▶		
16	Does the partnership have any foreign partners? If "Yes," enter the number of Forms 8805, Foreign Partner's Information Statement of Section 1446 Withholding Tax, filed for this partnership. ▶		
17	Enter the number of Forms 8865, Return of U.S. Persons With Respect to Certain Foreign Partnerships, attached to this return. ▶		
18a	Did you make any payments in 2017 that would require you to file Form(s) 1099? See instructions		
b	If "Yes," did you or will you file required Form(s) 1099?		
19	Enter the number of Form(s) 5471, Information Return of U.S. Persons With Respect To Certain Foreign Corporations, attached to this return. ▶		
20	Enter the number of partners that are foreign governments under section 892. ▶		
21	During the partnership's tax year, did the partnership make any payments that would require it to file Form 1042 and 1042-S under chapter 3 (sections 1441 through 1464) or chapter 4 (sections 1471 through 1474)?		
22	Was the partnership a specified domestic entity required to file Form 8938 for the tax year (See the Instructions for Form 8938)?		

Designation of Tax Matters Partner (see instructions)
Enter below the general partner or member-manager designated as the tax matters partner (TMP) for the tax year of this return:

Name of designated TMP ▶ _____   Identifying number of TMP ▶ _____

If the TMP is an entity, name of TMP representative ▶ _____   Phone number of TMP ▶ _____

Address of designated TMP ▶ _____

Form **1065** (2017)

Schedule K	Partners' Distributive Share Items		Total amount

				Total amount
Income (Loss)	1	Ordinary business income (loss) (page 1, line 22)	1	
	2	Net rental real estate income (loss) (attach Form 8825)	2	
	3a	Other gross rental income (loss)	3a	
	b	Expenses from other rental activities (attach statement)	3b	
	c	Other net rental income (loss). Subtract line 3b from line 3a	3c	
	4	Guaranteed payments	4	
	5	Interest income	5	
	6	Dividends: a Ordinary dividends	6a	
		b Qualified dividends	6b	
	7	Royalties	7	
	8	Net short-term capital gain (loss) (attach Schedule D (Form 1065))	8	
	9a	Net long-term capital gain (loss) (attach Schedule D (Form 1065))	9a	
	b	Collectibles (28%) gain (loss)	9b	
	c	Unrecaptured section 1250 gain (attach statement)	9c	
	10	Net section 1231 gain (loss) (attach Form 4797)	10	
	11	Other income (loss) (see instructions) Type ▶	11	
Deductions	12	Section 179 deduction (attach Form 4562)	12	
	13a	Contributions	13a	
	b	Investment interest expense	13b	
	c	Section 59(e)(2) expenditures: (1) Type ▶ (2) Amount ▶	13c(2)	
	d	Other deductions (see instructions) Type ▶	13d	
Self-Employment	14a	Net earnings (loss) from self-employment	14a	
	b	Gross farming or fishing income	14b	
	c	Gross nonfarm income	14c	
Credits	15a	Low-income housing credit (section 42(j)(5))	15a	
	b	Low-income housing credit (other)	15b	
	c	Qualified rehabilitation expenditures (rental real estate) (attach Form 3468, if applicable)	15c	
	d	Other rental real estate credits (see instructions) Type ▶	15d	
	e	Other rental credits (see instructions) Type ▶	15e	
	f	Other credits (see instructions) Type ▶	15f	
Foreign Transactions	16a	Name of country or U.S. possession ▶		
	b	Gross income from all sources	16b	
	c	Gross income sourced at partner level	16c	
		Foreign gross income sourced at partnership level		
	d	Passive category ▶ e General category ▶ f Other ▶	16f	
		Deductions allocated and apportioned at partner level		
	g	Interest expense ▶ h Other ▶	16h	
		Deductions allocated and apportioned at partnership level to foreign source income		
	i	Passive category ▶ j General category ▶ k Other ▶	16k	
	l	Total foreign taxes (check one): ▶ Paid ☐ Accrued ☐	16l	
	m	Reduction in taxes available for credit (attach statement)	16m	
	n	Other foreign tax information (attach statement)		
Alternative Minimum Tax (AMT) Items	17a	Post-1986 depreciation adjustment	17a	
	b	Adjusted gain or loss	17b	
	c	Depletion (other than oil and gas)	17c	
	d	Oil, gas, and geothermal properties—gross income	17d	
	e	Oil, gas, and geothermal properties—deductions	17e	
	f	Other AMT items (attach statement)	17f	
Other Information	18a	Tax-exempt interest income	18a	
	b	Other tax-exempt income	18b	
	c	Nondeductible expenses	18c	
	19a	Distributions of cash and marketable securities	19a	
	b	Distributions of other property	19b	
	20a	Investment income	20a	
	b	Investment expenses	20b	
	c	Other items and amounts (attach statement)		

Form **1065** (2017)

93

Analysis of Net Income (Loss)

1	Net income (loss). Combine Schedule K, lines 1 through 11. From the result, subtract the sum of Schedule K, lines 12 through 13d, and 16l					**1**		

2	Analysis by partner type:	(i) Corporate	(ii) Individual (active)	(iii) Individual (passive)	(iv) Partnership	(v) Exempt Organization	(vi) Nominee/Other
a	General partners						
b	Limited partners						

Schedule L — Balance Sheets per Books

	Assets	Beginning of tax year		End of tax year	
		(a)	(b)	(c)	(d)
1	Cash				
2a	Trade notes and accounts receivable . . .				
b	Less allowance for bad debts				
3	Inventories				
4	U.S. government obligations				
5	Tax-exempt securities				
6	Other current assets (attach statement) . .				
7a	Loans to partners (or persons related to partners)				
b	Mortgage and real estate loans . . .				
8	Other investments (attach statement) . . .				
9a	Buildings and other depreciable assets . .				
b	Less accumulated depreciation				
10a	Depletable assets				
b	Less accumulated depletion				
11	Land (net of any amortization)				
12a	Intangible assets (amortizable only) . . .				
b	Less accumulated amortization . . .				
13	Other assets (attach statement)				
14	Total assets				
	Liabilities and Capital				
15	Accounts payable				
16	Mortgages, notes, bonds payable in less than 1 year				
17	Other current liabilities (attach statement) .				
18	All nonrecourse loans				
19a	Loans from partners (or persons related to partners)				
b	Mortgages, notes, bonds payable in 1 year or more				
20	Other liabilities (attach statement) . . .				
21	Partners' capital accounts				
22	Total liabilities and capital				

Schedule M-1 — Reconciliation of Income (Loss) per Books With Income (Loss) per Return

Note. The partnership may be required to file Schedule M-3 (see instructions).

1	Net income (loss) per books		6	Income recorded on books this year not included on Schedule K, lines 1 through 11 (itemize):	
2	Income included on Schedule K, lines 1, 2, 3c, 5, 6a, 7, 8, 9a, 10, and 11, not recorded on books this year (itemize):		a	Tax-exempt interest $	
3	Guaranteed payments (other than health insurance)		7	Deductions included on Schedule K, lines 1 through 13d, and 16l, not charged against book income this year (itemize):	
4	Expenses recorded on books this year not included on Schedule K, lines 1 through 13d, and 16l (itemize):		a	Depreciation $	
a	Depreciation $				
b	Travel and entertainment $		8	Add lines 6 and 7	
5	Add lines 1 through 4		9	Income (loss) (Analysis of Net Income (Loss), line 1). Subtract line 8 from line 5 .	

Schedule M-2 — Analysis of Partners' Capital Accounts

1	Balance at beginning of year		6	Distributions: a Cash	
2	Capital contributed: a Cash . . .			b Property	
	b Property . .		7	Other decreases (itemize):	
3	Net income (loss) per books				
4	Other increases (itemize):		8	Add lines 6 and 7	
5	Add lines 1 through 4		9	Balance at end of year. Subtract line 8 from line 5	

Form **1065** (2017)

IRS Form 1065 (Schedule K-1) – Partner's Share of Income, Deductions, Credits, Etc.

Each partner is responsible for reporting their share of income, losses, deductions and credits on their individual tax return. This will be listed on the IRS form 1065 and will be listed through the partners income with the past-through business method. Each partner will then file a schedule K-1 with their tax returns.

| ☐ Final K-1 | ☐ Amended K-1 | OMB No. 1545-0123 |

Schedule K-1
(Form 1065)

Department of the Treasury
Internal Revenue Service

For calendar year 2017, or tax year

2017

beginning ___ / ___ / 2017   ending ___ / ___ / ___

Partner's Share of Income, Deductions, Credits, etc. ▶ See back of form and separate instructions.

Part I Information About the Partnership

A Partnership's employer identification number

B Partnership's name, address, city, state, and ZIP code

C IRS Center where partnership filed return

D ☐ Check if this is a publicly traded partnership (PTP)

Part II Information About the Partner

E Partner's identifying number

F Partner's name, address, city, state, and ZIP code

G ☐ General partner or LLC member-manager   ☐ Limited partner or other LLC member

H ☐ Domestic partner   ☐ Foreign partner

I1 What type of entity is this partner? _____

I2 If this partner is a retirement plan (IRA/SEP/Keogh/etc.), check here ☐

J Partner's share of profit, loss, and capital (see instructions):

	Beginning	Ending
Profit	%	%
Loss	%	%
Capital	%	%

K Partner's share of liabilities at year end:

Nonrecourse . . . . . . $ _____
Qualified nonrecourse financing . $ _____
Recourse . . . . $ _____

L Partner's capital account analysis:

Beginning capital account . . . $ _____
Capital contributed during the year $ _____
Current year increase (decrease) . $ _____
Withdrawals & distributions . . $ (_____)
Ending capital account . . . . $ _____

☐ Tax basis   ☐ GAAP   ☐ Section 704(b) book
☐ Other (explain) _____

M Did the partner contribute property with a built-in gain or loss?
☐ Yes   ☐ No
If "Yes," attach statement (see instructions)

Part III Partner's Share of Current Year Income, Deductions, Credits, and Other Items

1	Ordinary business income (loss)	15	Credits
2	Net rental real estate income (loss)		
3	Other net rental income (loss)	16	Foreign transactions
4	Guaranteed payments		
5	Interest income		
6a	Ordinary dividends		
6b	Qualified dividends		
7	Royalties		
8	Net short-term capital gain (loss)		
9a	Net long-term capital gain (loss)	17	Alternative minimum tax (AMT) items
9b	Collectibles (28%) gain (loss)		
9c	Unrecaptured section 1250 gain		
10	Net section 1231 gain (loss)	18	Tax-exempt income and nondeductible expenses
11	Other income (loss)		
		19	Distributions
12	Section 179 deduction		
13	Other deductions	20	Other information
14	Self-employment earnings (loss)		

*See attached statement for additional information.

For Paperwork Reduction Act Notice, see Instructions for Form 1065.   www.irs.gov/Form1065   Cat. No. 11394R   Schedule K-1 (Form 1065) 2017

This list identifies the codes used on Schedule K-1 for all partners and provides summarized reporting information for partners who file Form 1040. For detailed reporting and filing information, see the separate Partner's Instructions for Schedule K-1 and the instructions for your income tax return.

1. Ordinary business income (loss). Determine whether the income (loss) is passive or nonpassive and enter on your return as follows.

	Report on
Passive loss	See the Partner's Instructions
Passive income	Schedule E, line 28, column (g)
Nonpassive loss	See the Partner's Instructions
Nonpassive income	Schedule E, line 28, column (j)

2. Net rental real estate income (loss) See the Partner's Instructions

3. Other net rental income (loss)
Net income	Schedule E, line 28, column (g)
Net loss	See the Partner's Instructions

4. Guaranteed payments Schedule E, line 28, column (j)
5. Interest income Form 1040, line 8a
6a. Ordinary dividends Form 1040, line 9a
6b. Qualified dividends Form 1040, line 9b
7. Royalties Schedule E, line 4
8. Net short-term capital gain (loss) Schedule D, line 5
9a. Net long-term capital gain (loss) Schedule D, line 12
9b. Collectibles (28%) gain (loss) 28% Rate Gain Worksheet, line 4 (Schedule D instructions)
9c. Unrecaptured section 1250 gain See the Partner's Instructions
10. Net section 1231 gain (loss) See the Partner's Instructions
11. Other income (loss)

Code
A	Other portfolio income (loss)	See the Partner's Instructions
B	Involuntary conversions	See the Partner's Instructions
C	Sec. 1256 contracts & straddles	Form 6781, line 1
D	Mining exploration costs recapture	See Pub. 535
E	Cancellation of debt	Form 1040, line 21 or Form 982
F	Other income (loss)	See the Partner's Instructions

12. Section 179 deduction See the Partner's Instructions
13. Other deductions
A	Cash contributions (50%)	
B	Cash contributions (30%)	
C	Noncash contributions (50%)	
D	Noncash contributions (30%)	See the Partner's Instructions
E	Capital gain property to a 50% organization (30%)	
F	Capital gain property (20%)	
G	Contributions (100%)	
H	Investment interest expense	Form 4952, line 1
I	Deductions—royalty income	Schedule E, line 19
J	Section 59(e)(2) expenditures	See the Partner's Instructions
K	Deductions—portfolio (2% floor)	Schedule A, line 23
L	Deductions—portfolio (other)	Schedule A, line 28
M	Amounts paid for medical insurance	Schedule A, line 1 or Form 1040, line 29
N	Educational assistance benefits	See the Partner's Instructions
O	Dependent care benefits	Form 2441, line 12
P	Preproductive period expenses	See the Partner's Instructions
Q	Commercial revitalization deduction from rental real estate activities	See Form 8582 instructions
R	Pensions and IRAs	See the Partner's Instructions
S	Reforestation expense deduction	See the Partner's Instructions
T	Domestic production activities information	See Form 8903 instructions
U	Qualified production activities income	Form 8903, line 7b
V	Employer's Form W-2 wages	Form 8903, line 17
W	Other deductions	See the Partner's Instructions

14. Self-employment earnings (loss)

Note: If you have a section 179 deduction or any partner-level deductions, see the Partner's Instructions before completing Schedule SE.
A	Net earnings (loss) from self-employment	Schedule SE, Section A or B
B	Gross farming or fishing income	See the Partner's Instructions
C	Gross non-farm income	See the Partner's Instructions

15. Credits
A	Low-income housing credit (section 42(j)(5)) from pre-2008 buildings	
B	Low-income housing credit (other) from pre-2008 buildings	
C	Low-income housing credit (section 42(j)(5)) from post-2007 buildings	
D	Low-income housing credit (other) from post-2007 buildings	See the Partner's Instructions
E	Qualified rehabilitation expenditures (rental real estate)	
F	Other rental real estate credits	
G	Other rental credits	
H	Undistributed capital gains credit	Form 1040, line 73; check box a
I	Biofuel producer credit	
J	Work opportunity credit	See the Partner's Instructions
K	Disabled access credit	

Code
L	Empowerment zone employment credit	
M	Credit for increasing research activities	
N	Credit for employer social security and Medicare taxes	See the Partner's Instructions
O	Backup withholding	
P	Other credits	

16. Foreign transactions
A	Name of country or U.S. possession	
B	Gross income from all sources	Form 1116, Part I
C	Gross income sourced at partner level	

Foreign gross income sourced at partnership level
D	Passive category	
E	General category	Form 1116, Part I
F	Other	

Deductions allocated and apportioned at partner level
G	Interest expense	Form 1116, Part I
H	Other	Form 1116, Part I

Deductions allocated and apportioned at partnership level to foreign source income
I	Passive category	
J	General category	Form 1116, Part I
K	Other	

Other information
L	Total foreign taxes paid	Form 1116, Part II
M	Total foreign taxes accrued	Form 1116, Part II
N	Reduction in taxes available for credit	Form 1116, line 12
O	Foreign trading gross receipts	Form 8873
P	Extraterritorial income exclusion	Form 8873
Q	Other foreign transactions	See the Partner's Instructions

17. Alternative minimum tax (AMT) items
A	Post-1986 depreciation adjustment	
B	Adjusted gain or loss	See the Partner's
C	Depletion (other than oil & gas)	Instructions and
D	Oil, gas, & geothermal—gross income	the Instructions for
E	Oil, gas, & geothermal—deductions	Form 6251
F	Other AMT items	

18. Tax-exempt income and nondeductible expenses
A	Tax-exempt interest income	Form 1040, line 8b
B	Other tax-exempt income	See the Partner's Instructions
C	Nondeductible expenses	See the Partner's Instructions

19. Distributions
A	Cash and marketable securities	
B	Distribution subject to section 737	See the Partner's Instructions
C	Other property	

20. Other information
A	Investment income	Form 4952, line 4a
B	Investment expenses	Form 4952, line 5
C	Fuel tax credit information	Form 4136
D	Qualified rehabilitation expenditures (other than rental real estate)	See the Partner's Instructions
E	Basis of energy property	See the Partner's Instructions
F	Recapture of low-income housing credit (section 42(j)(5))	Form 8611, line 8
G	Recapture of low-income housing credit (other)	Form 8611, line 8
H	Recapture of investment credit	See Form 4255
I	Recapture of other credits	See the Partner's Instructions
J	Look-back interest—completed long-term contracts	See Form 8697
K	Look-back interest—income forecast method	See Form 8866
L	Dispositions of property with section 179 deductions	
M	Recapture of section 179 deduction	
N	Interest expense for corporate partners	
O	Section 453(l)(3) information	
P	Section 453A(c) information	
Q	Section 1260(b) information	
R	Interest allocable to production expenditures	See the Partner's Instructions
S	CCF nonqualified withdrawals	
T	Depletion information—oil and gas	
U	Reserved	
V	Unrelated business taxable income	
W	Precontribution gain (loss)	
X	Section 108(i) information	
Y	Net investment income	
Z	Other information	

IRS Form 1096 – Annual Summary and Transmittal of U.S. Information Returns

A form 1096 will be used if your organization is tax-exempt.

Form **1096**

Department of the Treasury
Internal Revenue Service

Do Not Staple 6969

Annual Summary and Transmittal of U.S. Information Returns

OMB No. 1545-0108

2017

FILER'S name

Street address (including room or suite number)

City or town, state or province, country, and ZIP or foreign postal code

Name of person to contact

Telephone number

Email address

Fax number

For Official Use Only

1 Employer identification number	2 Social security number	3 Total number of forms	4 Federal income tax withheld	5 Total amount reported with this Form 1096
			$	$

6 Enter an "X" in only one box below to indicate the type of form being filed.
7 Form 1099-MISC with NEC in box 7, check . . . . . ▸ ☐

W-2G 32	1097-BTC 50	1098 81	1098-C 78	1098-E 84	1098-Q 74	1098-T 83	1099-A 80	1099-B 79	1099-C 85	1099-CAP 73	1099-DIV 91	1099-G 86	1099-INT 92	1099-K 10
☐	☐	☐	☐	☐	☐	☐	☐	☐	☐	☐	☐	☐	☐	☐

1099-LTC 93	1099-MISC 95	1099-OID 96	1099-PATR 97	1099-Q 31	1099-QA 1A	1099-R 98	1099-S 75	1099-SA 94	3921 25	3922 26	5498 28	5498-ESA 72	5498-QA 2A	5498-SA 27
☐	☐	☐	☐	☐	☐	☐	☐	☐	☐	☐	☐	☐	☐	☐

Return this entire page to the Internal Revenue Service. Photocopies are not acceptable.

Under penalties of perjury, I declare that I have examined this return and accompanying documents, and, to the best of my knowledge and belief, they are true, correct, and complete.

Signature ▸

Title ▸

Date ▸

Instructions

Future developments. For the latest information about developments related to Form 1096, such as legislation enacted after it was published, go to www.irs.gov/form1096.

Reminder. The only acceptable method of electronically filing information returns listed on this form in box 6 with the IRS is through the FIRE system. See Pub. 1220.

Purpose of form. Use this form to transmit paper Forms 1097, 1098, 1099, 3921, 3922, 5498, and W-2G to the Internal Revenue Service.

Caution: If you are required to file 250 or more information returns of any one type, you must file electronically. If you are required to file electronically but fail to do so, and you do not have an approved waiver, you may be subject to a penalty. For more information, see part F in the 2017 General Instructions for Certain Information Returns.

Forms 1099-QA and 5498-QA can be filed on paper only, regardless of the number of returns.

Who must file. The name, address, and TIN of the filer on this form must be the same as those you enter in the upper left area of Forms 1097, 1098, 1099, 3921, 3922, 5498, or W-2G. A filer is any person or entity who files any of the forms shown in line 6 above.

Enter the filer's name, address (including room, suite, or other unit number), and TIN in the spaces provided on the form.

When to file. File Form 1096 as follows.

• With Forms 1097, 1098, 1099, 3921, 3922, or W-2G, file by February 28, 2018.

Caution: File Form 1099-MISC by January 31, 2018, if you are reporting **nonemployee compensation** in box 7. Also, check box 7 above.

• With Forms 5498, file by May 31, 2018.

Where To File

Send all information returns filed on paper with Form 1096 to the following.

If your principal business, office or agency, or legal residence in the case of an individual, is located in	Use the following three-line address
Alabama, Arizona, Arkansas, Connecticut, Delaware, Florida, Georgia, Kentucky, Louisiana, Maine, Massachusetts, Mississippi, New Hampshire, New Jersey, New Mexico, New York, North Carolina, Ohio, Pennsylvania, Rhode Island, Texas, Vermont, Virginia, West Virginia	Department of the Treasury Internal Revenue Service Center Austin, TX 73301

For more information and the Privacy Act and Paperwork Reduction Act Notice, see the 2017 General Instructions for Certain Information Returns.

Cat. No. 14400O

Form **1096** (2017)

IRS Form 1099-MISC – Miscellaneous Income (Contractors)

Form 1099-MISC is a report of miscellaneous payments that are made to those who are not regular employees. This would include freelancers, independent contractors, etc. based on those you used during the calendar year.

☐ VOID ☐ CORRECTED		

PAYER'S name, street address, city or town, state or province, country, ZIP or foreign postal code, and telephone no.	1 Rents $	OMB No. 1545-0115
	2 Royalties $	2018 Form 1099-MISC	Miscellaneous Income
	3 Other income $	4 Federal income tax withheld $	Copy 1
PAYER'S TIN	RECIPIENT'S TIN	5 Fishing boat proceeds $	6 Medical and health care payments $	For State Tax Department
RECIPIENT'S name	7 Nonemployee compensation $	8 Substitute payments in lieu of dividends or interest $
Street address (including apt. no.)	9 Payer made direct sales of $5,000 or more of consumer products to a buyer (recipient) for resale ☐	10 Crop insurance proceeds $
City or town, state or province, country, and ZIP or foreign postal code	11	12
Account number (see instructions)	FATCA filing requirement ☐	13 Excess golden parachute payments $	14 Gross proceeds paid to an attorney $
15a Section 409A deferrals $	15b Section 409A income $	16 State tax withheld $	17 State/Payer's state no.	18 State income $

Form **1099-MISC**   www.irs.gov/Form1099MISC   Department of the Treasury - Internal Revenue Service

IRS Form 5695 – Residential Energy Credit

If you have made your property energy efficient, you will fill out this form to receive the nonbusiness energy property credit and the residential energy efficient property credit.

Form 5695

Department of the Treasury
Internal Revenue Service

Residential Energy Credit

▶ Go to www.irs.gov/Form5695 for instructions and the latest information.
▶ Attach to Form 1040 or Form 1040NR.

OMB No. 1545-0074

2017

Attachment
Sequence No. **158**

Name(s) shown on return

Your social security number

Part I	**Residential Energy Efficient Property Credit** (See instructions before completing this part.)	

Note: Skip lines 1 through 11 if you only have a **credit carryforward from 2016.**

1	Qualified solar electric property costs	1	
2	Qualified solar water heating property costs	2	
3	Reserved for future use	3	
4	Reserved for future use	4	
5	Add lines 1 and 2	5	
6	Multiply line 5 by 30% (0.30)	6	
7a	Reserved for future use ▶	7a	
b	Reserved for future use		
8	Reserved for future use	8	
9	Reserved for future use	9	
10	Reserved for future use	10	
11	Reserved for future use	11	
12	Credit carryforward from 2016. Enter the amount, if any, from your 2016 Form 5695, line 16	12	
13	Add lines 6 and 12	13	
14	Limitation based on tax liability. Enter the amount from the Residential Energy Efficient Property Credit Limit Worksheet. See instructions	14	
15	**Residential energy efficient property credit.** Enter the smaller of line 13 or line 14. Also include this amount on Form 1040, line 53; or Form 1040NR, line 50	15	
16	Credit carryforward to 2018. If line 15 is less than line 13, subtract line 15 from line 13	16	

For Paperwork Reduction Act Notice, see your tax return instructions.   Cat. No. 13540P   Form **5695** (2017)

IRS Form 6251 – Alternative Minimum Tax (Individuals)

If you qualify for the Alternative Minimum Tax and need to calculate that into your tax return, you can use form 6251.

Form 6251

Alternative Minimum Tax—Individuals

Department of the Treasury
Internal Revenue Service (99)

▶ Go to www.irs.gov/Form6251 for instructions and the latest information.
▶ Attach to Form 1040 or Form 1040NR.

OMB No. 1545-0074

2017

Attachment
Sequence No. 32

Name(s) shown on Form 1040 or Form 1040NR

Your social security number

Part I — Alternative Minimum Taxable Income (See instructions for how to complete each line.)

1	If filing Schedule A (Form 1040), enter the amount from Form 1040, line 41, and go to line 2. Otherwise, enter the amount from Form 1040, line 38, and go to line 7. (If less than zero, enter as a negative amount.)	1
2	Reserved for future use	2
3	Taxes from Schedule A (Form 1040), line 9	3
4	Enter the home mortgage interest adjustment, if any, from line 6 of the worksheet in the instructions for this line	4
5	Miscellaneous deductions from Schedule A (Form 1040), line 27	5
6	If Form 1040, line 38, is $156,900 or less, enter -0-. Otherwise, see instructions	6 ( )
7	Tax refund from Form 1040, line 10 or line 21	7 ( )
8	Investment interest expense (difference between regular tax and AMT)	8
9	Depletion (difference between regular tax and AMT)	9
10	Net operating loss deduction from Form 1040, line 21. Enter as a positive amount	10
11	Alternative tax net operating loss deduction	11 ( )
12	Interest from specified private activity bonds exempt from the regular tax	12
13	Qualified small business stock, see instructions	13
14	Exercise of incentive stock options (excess of AMT income over regular tax income)	14
15	Estates and trusts (amount from Schedule K-1 (Form 1041), box 12, code A)	15
16	Electing large partnerships (amount from Schedule K-1 (Form 1065-B), box 6)	16
17	Disposition of property (difference between AMT and regular tax gain or loss)	17
18	Depreciation on assets placed in service after 1986 (difference between regular tax and AMT)	18
19	Passive activities (difference between AMT and regular tax income or loss)	19
20	Loss limitations (difference between AMT and regular tax income or loss)	20
21	Circulation costs (difference between regular tax and AMT)	21
22	Long-term contracts (difference between AMT and regular tax income)	22
23	Mining costs (difference between regular tax and AMT)	23
24	Research and experimental costs (difference between regular tax and AMT)	24
25	Income from certain installment sales before January 1, 1987	25 ( )
26	Intangible drilling costs preference	26
27	Other adjustments, including income-based related adjustments	27
28	**Alternative minimum taxable income.** Combine lines 1 through 27. (If married filing separately and line 28 is more than $249,450, see instructions.)	28

Part II — Alternative Minimum Tax (AMT)

29 Exemption. (If you were under age 24 at the end of 2017, see instructions.)

IF your filing status is . . .	AND line 28 is not over . . .	THEN enter on line 29 . . .	
Single or head of household	$120,700	$54,300	
Married filing jointly or qualifying widow(er)	160,900	84,500	
Married filing separately	80,450	42,250	

If line 28 is **over** the amount shown above for your filing status, see instructions.

29	

30 Subtract line 29 from line 28. If more than zero, go to line 31. If zero or less, enter -0- here and on lines 31, 33, and 35, and go to line 34 — **30**

31
- If you are filing Form 2555 or 2555-EZ, see instructions for the amount to enter.
- If you reported capital gain distributions directly on Form 1040, line 13; you reported qualified dividends on Form 1040, line 9b; or you had a gain on both lines 15 and 16 of Schedule D (Form 1040) (as refigured for the AMT, if necessary), complete Part III on the back and enter the amount from line 64 here.
- All others: If line 30 is $187,800 or less ($93,900 or less if married filing separately), multiply line 30 by 26% (0.26). Otherwise, multiply line 30 by 28% (0.28) and subtract $3,756 ($1,878 if married filing separately) from the result. — **31**

32 Alternative minimum tax foreign tax credit (see instructions) — **32**

33 Tentative minimum tax. Subtract line 32 from line 31 — **33**

34 Add Form 1040, line 44 (minus any tax from Form 4972), and Form 1040, line 46. Subtract from the result any foreign tax credit from Form 1040, line 48. If you used Schedule J to figure your tax on Form 1040, line 44, refigure that tax without using Schedule J before completing this line (see instructions) — **34**

35 **AMT.** Subtract line 34 from line 33. If zero or less, enter -0-. Enter here and on Form 1040, line 45 — **35**

For Paperwork Reduction Act Notice, see your tax return instructions.   Cat. No. 13000G   Form **6251** (2017)

101

Part III **Tax Computation Using Maximum Capital Gains Rates**

Complete Part III only if you are required to do so by line 31 or by the Foreign Earned Income Tax Worksheet in the instructions.

36 Enter the amount from Form 6251, line 30. If you are filing Form 2555 or 2555-EZ, enter the amount from line 3 of the worksheet in the instructions for line 31	36	
37 Enter the amount from line 6 of the Qualified Dividends and Capital Gain Tax Worksheet in the instructions for Form 1040, line 44, or the amount from line 13 of the Schedule D Tax Worksheet in the instructions for Schedule D (Form 1040), whichever applies (as refigured for the AMT, if necessary) (see instructions). If you are filing Form 2555 or 2555-EZ, see instructions for the amount to enter	37	
38 Enter the amount from Schedule D (Form 1040), line 19 (as refigured for the AMT, if necessary) (see instructions). If you are filing Form 2555 or 2555-EZ, see instructions for the amount to enter	38	
39 If you did not complete a Schedule D Tax Worksheet for the regular tax or the AMT, enter the amount from line 37. Otherwise, add lines 37 and 38, and enter the **smaller** of that result or the amount from line 10 of the Schedule D Tax Worksheet (as refigured for the AMT, if necessary). If you are filing Form 2555 or 2555-EZ, see instructions for the amount to enter	39	
40 Enter the **smaller** of line 36 or line 39	40	
41 Subtract line 40 from line 38	41	
42 If line 41 is $187,800 or less ($93,900 or less if married filing separately), multiply line 41 by 26% (0.26). Otherwise, multiply line 41 by 28% (0.28) and subtract $3,756 ($1,878 if married filing separately) from the result ▶	42	
43 Enter: • $75,900 if married filing jointly or qualifying widow(er), • $37,950 if single or married filing separately, or • $50,800 if head of household.	43	
44 Enter the amount from line 7 of the Qualified Dividends and Capital Gain Tax Worksheet in the instructions for Form 1040, line 44, or the amount from line 14 of the Schedule D Tax Worksheet in the instructions for Schedule D (Form 1040), whichever applies (as figured for the regular tax). If you did not complete either worksheet for the regular tax, enter the amount from Form 1040, line 43; if zero or less, enter -0-. If you are filing Form 2555 or 2555-EZ, see instructions for the amount to enter	44	
45 Subtract line 44 from line 43. If zero or less, enter -0-	45	
46 Enter the **smaller** of line 36 or line 37	46	
47 Enter the **smaller** of line 45 or line 46. This amount is taxed at 0%	47	
48 Subtract line 47 from line 46	48	
49 Enter: • $418,400 if single • $235,350 if married filing separately • $470,700 if married filing jointly or qualifying widow(er) • $444,550 if head of household	49	
50 Enter the amount from line 45	50	
51 Enter the amount from line 7 of the Qualified Dividends and Capital Gain Tax Worksheet in the instructions for Form 1040, line 44, or the amount from line 19 of the Schedule D Tax Worksheet, whichever applies (as figured for the regular tax). If you did not complete either worksheet for the regular tax, enter the amount from Form 1040, line 43; if zero or less, enter -0-. If you are filing Form 2555 or Form 2555-EZ, see instructions for the amount to enter	51	
52 Add line 50 and line 51	52	
53 Subtract line 52 from line 49. If zero or less, enter -0-	53	
54 Enter the smaller of line 48 or line 53	54	
55 Multiply line 54 by 15% (0.15) . . . . ▶	55	
56 Add lines 47 and 54	56	
If lines 56 and 36 are the same, skip lines 57 through 61 and go to line 62. Otherwise, go to line 57.		
57 Subtract line 56 from line 46	57	
58 Multiply line 57 by 20% (0.20) . . . . ▶	58	
If line 38 is zero or blank, skip lines 59 through 61 and go to line 62. Otherwise, go to line 59.		
59 Add lines 41, 56, and 57	59	
60 Subtract line 59 from line 36	60	
61 Multiply line 60 by 25% (0.25) . . . . ▶	61	
62 Add lines 42, 55, 58, and 61	62	
63 If line 36 is $187,800 or less ($93,900 or less if married filing separately), multiply line 36 by 26% (0.26). Otherwise, multiply line 36 by 28% (0.28) and subtract $3,756 ($1,878 if married filing separately) from the result	63	
64 Enter the **smaller** of line 62 or line 63 here and on line 31. If you are filing Form 2555 or 2555-EZ, do not enter this amount on line 31. Instead, enter it on line 4 of the worksheet in the instructions for line 31 . .	64	

Form **6251** (2017)

IRS Form 8109 – Federal Tax Deposit Coupon

All businesses will be familiar with form 8109. This form is used for tax filing and reporting purposes. It will be used to make deposits for payroll, corporate income, or other forms of taxes.

SEPARATE ALONG THIS LINE AND SUBMIT TO DEPOSITARY WITH PAYMENT

OMB NO. 1545-0257

IMPORTANT
Read instructions carefully before completing Form 8109-B, Federal Tax Deposit Coupon.

Note: *Except for the name, address, and telephone number, entries are processed by optical scanning equipment and must be made in pencil. Please use a soft lead (for example, a #2 pencil) so that the entries can be read more accurately by the optical scanning equipment. The name, address, and telephone number may be completed other than by hand. You CANNOT use photocopies of live coupons to make your deposits. DO NOT staple, tape or fold the coupons.*

Schedule A, Form 941 Filers (4th quarter 1993 ONLY).—If you are making a deposit for the 4th quarter 1993 during January 1994, darken the **945 box** under TYPE OF TAX and the **4th quarter box** under TAX PERIOD.

Paperwork Reduction Act Notice.—We ask for the information on this form to carry out the Internal Revenue laws of the United States. You are required to give us the information. We need it to ensure that you are complying with these laws and to allow us to figure and collect the right amount of tax.

The time needed to complete and file this form will vary depending on individual circumstances. The estimated average time is 3 min. If you have comments concerning the accuracy of this time estimate or suggestions for making this form more simple, we would be happy to hear from you. You can write to both the **Internal Revenue Service**, Attention: Reports Clearance Officer, PC:FP, Washington, DC 20224; and the **Office of Management and Budget**, Paperwork Reduction Project (1545-0257), Washington, DC 20503. **DO NOT** send this form to either of these offices. Instead, see the instructions on the back of this page.

Purpose of Form.—Use Form 8109-B deposit coupons to make tax deposits **only** in the following two situations:

1. You have not yet received your resupply of preprinted deposit coupons (Form 8109); or

2. You are a new entity and have already been assigned an employer identification number (EIN), but have not yet received your initial supply of preprinted deposit coupons (Form 8109).

Note: *If you do not receive your resupply of deposit coupons and a deposit is due or you do not receive your initial supply within 5-6 weeks of receipt of your EIN, please contact your local IRS office.*

If you have applied for an EIN, have not received it, and a deposit must be made, send your payment to your Internal Revenue Service Center. Make your check or money order payable to the Internal Revenue Service and show on it your name (as shown on **Form SS-4**, Application for Employer Identification Number), address, kind of tax, period covered, and date you applied for an EIN. Also attach an explanation to the deposit. Do **NOT** use Form 8109-B in this situation. Do **NOT** use Form 8109-B to deposit delinquent taxes assessed by the IRS. Pay those taxes directly to the IRS.

How To Complete the Form.—Enter your name exactly as shown on your return or other IRS correspondence, address, and EIN in the spaces provided. If you are required to file a Form 1120, 990-C, 990-PF (with net investment income), 990-T, or 2438, enter the month in which your tax year ends in the **TAX YEAR MONTH** boxes. For example, if your tax years ends in January, enter 01; if it ends in June, enter 06; if it ends in December, enter 12. Please make your entries for EIN and tax year month (if applicable) in the manner specified in Amount of Deposit below. Darken one box each in the Type of Tax and Tax Period columns as explained below.

Amount of Deposit.—Enter the amount of the deposit in the space provided. Enter the amount legibly, forming the characters as shown below:

1 2 3 4 5 6 7 8 9 0

Hand-print money amounts without using dollar signs, commas, a decimal point, or leading zeros. The commas and the decimal point are already shown in the entry area. For example, a deposit of $7,635.22 would be entered like this:

		DOLLARS		CENTS
		7 6 3 5		2 2

If the deposit is for whole dollars only, enter "00" in the CENTS boxes.

Types of Tax.—

Form 941	—Withheld Income From Wages and Other Compensation, Social Security, and Medicare Taxes (includes Form 941 series of returns)
Form 945	—Withheld Income Tax From Pension, Annuities, Gambling, and Backup Withholding.
Form 990-C	—Farmers' Cooperative Association Income Tax.
Form 943	—Agricultural Withheld Income, Social Security, and Medicare Taxes (includes Form 943PR).
Form 720	—Excise Tax.
Form CT-1	—Railroad Retirement and Railroad Unemployment Repayment Taxes.
Form 940	—Federal Unemployment (FUTA) Tax (includes Form 940-EZ and Form 940PR).
Form 1120	—Corporate Income Tax (includes Form 1120 series of returns and Form 2438).
Form 990-T	—Exempt Organization Business Income Tax.

Form 990-PF ...—Excise Tax on Private Foundation Net Investment Income.

Form 1042 ...—Withholding On Foreign Persons.

How To Determine the Proper Tax Period.—

Payroll Taxes and Withholding (Forms 941, 940, 943, 945, CT-1, and 1042. (See the separate instructions for Form 1042. **Schedule A (Form 941) filers see information above.)**).

If your liability was incurred during:

• January 1 through March 31, darken the 1st quarter box
• April 1 through June 30, darken the 2nd quarter box
• July 1 through September 30, darken the 3rd quarter box
• October 1 through December 31, darken the 4th quarter box

Note: If the liability was incurred during one quarter and deposited in another, darken the box for the quarter in which the tax liability was incurred. For example, if the liability was incurred in March and deposited in April, darken the 1st quarter box.

(Continued on back of page.)

Department of the Treasury
Internal Revenue Service

Cat. No. 61042S

Form **8109-B** (Rev. 1-94)

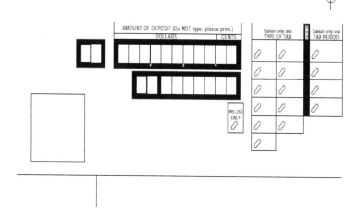

IRS Form 8949 – Sales and Other Dispositions of Capital Assets

Before you can fill out the form 1040 (Schedule D), you first need to fill out form 8949. This will help you with the breakdown of your sales and give you some important information that is needed on the schedule D.

Form **8949**

Department of the Treasury
Internal Revenue Service

OMB No. 1545-0074

Sales and Other Dispositions of Capital Assets

▶ Go to www.irs.gov/Form8949 for instructions and the latest information.

▶ File with your Schedule D to list your transactions for lines 1b, 2, 3, 8b, 9, and 10 of Schedule D.

2017

Attachment
Sequence No. **12A**

Name(s) shown on return

Social security number or taxpayer identification number

Before you check Box A, B, or C below, see whether you received any Form(s) 1099-B or substitute statement(s) from your broker. A substitute statement will have the same information as Form 1099-B. Either will show whether your basis (usually your cost) was reported to the IRS by your broker and may even tell you which box to check.

Part I **Short-Term.** Transactions involving capital assets you held 1 year or less are short term. For long-term transactions, see page 2.

> **Note:** You may aggregate all short-term transactions reported on Form(s) 1099-B showing basis was reported to the IRS and for which no adjustments or codes are required. Enter the totals directly on Schedule D, line 1a; you aren't required to report these transactions on Form 8949 (see instructions).

You must check Box A, B, or C below. Check only one box. If more than one box applies for your short-term transactions, complete a separate Form 8949, page 1, for each applicable box. If you have more short-term transactions than will fit on this page for one or more of the boxes, complete as many forms with the same box checked as you need.

- ☐ **(A)** Short-term transactions reported on Form(s) 1099-B showing basis was reported to the IRS (see **Note** above)
- ☐ **(B)** Short-term transactions reported on Form(s) 1099-B showing basis **wasn't** reported to the IRS
- ☐ **(C)** Short-term transactions not reported to you on Form 1099-B

1	(a) Description of property (Example: 100 sh. XYZ Co.)	(b) Date acquired (Mo., day, yr.)	(c) Date sold or disposed of (Mo., day, yr.)	(d) Proceeds (sales price) (see instructions)	(e) Cost or other basis. See the **Note** below and see Column (e) in the separate instructions	Adjustment, if any, to gain or loss. If you enter an amount in column (g), enter a code in column (f). See the separate instructions.		(h) Gain or (loss). Subtract column (e) from column (d) and combine the result with column (g)
						(f) Code(s) from instructions	(g) Amount of adjustment	
2 Totals. Add the amounts in columns (d), (e), (g), and (h) (subtract negative amounts). Enter each total here and include on your Schedule D, **line 1b** (if Box A above is checked), **line 2** (if Box B above is checked), or **line 3** (if Box C above is checked) ▶								

Note: If you checked Box A above but the basis reported to the IRS was incorrect, enter in column (e) the basis as reported to the IRS, and enter an adjustment in column (g) to correct the basis. See Column (g) in the separate instructions for how to figure the amount of the adjustment.

For Paperwork Reduction Act Notice, see your tax return instructions.

Cat. No. 37768Z

Form **8949** (2017)

Name(s) shown on return. Name and SSN or taxpayer identification no. not required if shown on other side	Social security number or taxpayer identification number

Before you check Box D, E, or F below, see whether you received any Form(s) 1099-B or substitute statement(s) from your broker. A substitute statement will have the same information as Form 1099-B. Either will show whether your basis (usually your cost) was reported to the IRS by your broker and may even tell you which box to check.

Part II **Long-Term.** Transactions involving capital assets you held more than 1 year are long term. For short-term transactions, see page 1.

Note: You may aggregate all long-term transactions reported on Form(s) 1099-B showing basis was reported to the IRS and for which no adjustments or codes are required. Enter the totals directly on Schedule D, line 8a; you aren't required to report these transactions on Form 8949 (see instructions).

You must check Box D, E, or F below. Check only one box. If more than one box applies for your long-term transactions, complete a separate Form 8949, page 2, for each applicable box. If you have more long-term transactions than will fit on this page for one or more of the boxes, complete as many forms with the same box checked as you need.

- ☐ **(D)** Long-term transactions reported on Form(s) 1099-B showing basis was reported to the IRS (see **Note** above)
- ☐ **(E)** Long-term transactions reported on Form(s) 1099-B showing basis **wasn't** reported to the IRS
- ☐ **(F)** Long-term transactions not reported to you on Form 1099-B

1						Adjustment, if any, to gain or loss. If you enter an amount in column (g), enter a code in column (f). See the separate instructions.		
(a) Description of property (Example: 100 sh. XYZ Co.)	(b) Date acquired (Mo., day, yr.)	(c) Date sold or disposed of (Mo., day, yr.)	(d) Proceeds (sales price) (see instructions)	(e) Cost or other basis. See the Note below and see Column (e) in the separate instructions	(f) Code(s) from instructions	(g) Amount of adjustment	(h) Gain or (loss). Subtract column (e) from column (d) and combine the result with column (g)
2 Totals. Add the amounts in columns (d), (e), (g), and (h) (subtract negative amounts). Enter each total here and include on your Schedule D, **line 8b** (if **Box D** above is checked), **line 9** (if **Box E** above is checked), or **line 10** (if **Box F** above is checked) ▶							

Note: If you checked Box D above but the basis reported to the IRS was incorrect, enter in column (e) the basis as reported to the IRS, and enter an adjustment in column (g) to correct the basis. See Column (g) in the separate instructions for how to figure the amount of the adjustment.

Form **8949** (2017)

IRS Form 8960 – Net Investment Income Tax (Individuals, Estates and Trust)

Form 8960 will be used to report your net investment income tax. That means any income you bring in from investments will be reported with this form.

Form **8960**	Net Investment Income Tax— Individuals, Estates, and Trusts	OMB No. 1545-2227
Department of the Treasury Internal Revenue Service (99)	▶ Attach to your tax return. ▶ Go to www.irs.gov/Form8960 for instructions and the latest information.	**2017** Attachment Sequence No. **72**

Name(s) shown on your tax return | Your social security number or EIN

Part I   Investment Income   ☐ Section 6013(g) election (see instructions)
                                         ☐ Section 6013(h) election (see instructions)
                                         ☐ Regulations section 1.1411-10(g) election (see instructions)

1	Taxable interest (see instructions)	**1**
2	Ordinary dividends (see instructions)	**2**
3	Annuities (see instructions)	**3**
4a	Rental real estate, royalties, partnerships, S corporations, trusts, etc. (see instructions)	**4a**
b	Adjustment for net income or loss derived in the ordinary course of a non-section 1411 trade or business (see instructions)	**4b**
c	Combine lines 4a and 4b	**4c**
5a	Net gain or loss from disposition of property (see instructions)	**5a**
b	Net gain or loss from disposition of property that is not subject to net investment income tax (see instructions)	**5b**
c	Adjustment from disposition of partnership interest or S corporation stock (see instructions)	**5c**
d	Combine lines 5a through 5c	**5d**
6	Adjustments to investment income for certain CFCs and PFICs (see instructions)	**6**
7	Other modifications to investment income (see instructions)	**7**
8	Total investment income. Combine lines 1, 2, 3, 4c, 5d, 6, and 7	**8**

Part II   Investment Expenses Allocable to Investment Income and Modifications

9a	Investment interest expenses (see instructions)	**9a**
b	State, local, and foreign income tax (see instructions)	**9b**
c	Miscellaneous investment expenses (see instructions)	**9c**
d	Add lines 9a, 9b, and 9c	**9d**
10	Additional modifications (see instructions)	**10**
11	Total deductions and modifications. Add lines 9d and 10	**11**

Part III   Tax Computation

12	Net investment income. Subtract Part II, line 11 from Part I, line 8. Individuals complete lines 13–17. Estates and trusts complete lines 18a–21. If zero or less, enter -0-	**12**

Individuals:

13	Modified adjusted gross income (see instructions)	**13**
14	Threshold based on filing status (see instructions)	**14**
15	Subtract line 14 from line 13. If zero or less, enter -0-	**15**
16	Enter the smaller of line 12 or line 15	**16**
17	Net investment income tax for individuals. Multiply line 16 by 3.8% (.038). **Enter here and include on your tax return** (see instructions)	**17**

Estates and Trusts:

18a	Net investment income (line 12 above)	**18a**
b	Deductions for distributions of net investment income and deductions under section 642(c) (see instructions)	**18b**
c	Undistributed net investment income. Subtract line 18b from 18a (see instructions). If zero or less, enter -0-	**18c**
19a	Adjusted gross income (see instructions)	**19a**
b	Highest tax bracket for estates and trusts for the year (see instructions)	**19b**
c	Subtract line 19b from line 19a. If zero or less, enter -0-	**19c**
20	Enter the smaller of line 18c or line 19c	**20**
21	Net investment income tax for estates and trusts. Multiply line 20 by 3.8% (.038). **Enter here and include on your tax return** (see instructions)	**21**

For Paperwork Reduction Act Notice, see your tax return instructions.   Cat. No. 59474M   Form **8960** (2017)

IRS Form I-9 – Employment Eligibility Verification

When you work in the United States, form I-9 is required by both the employers and the employees. It will establish if you are authorized to work in the United States.

Department of Homeland Security
U.S. Citizenship and Immigration Services

Form I-9, Employment
Eligibility Verification

Read instructions carefully before completing this form. The instructions must be available during completion of this form.

ANTI-DISCRIMINATION NOTICE: It is illegal to discriminate against work-authorized individuals. Employers CANNOT specify which document(s) they will accept from an employee. The refusal to hire an individual because the documents have a future expiration date may also constitute illegal discrimination.

Section 1. Employee Information and Verification *(To be completed and signed by employee at the time employment begins.)*

Print Name: Last	First	Middle Initial	Maiden Name

Address *(Street Name and Number)*		Apt. #	Date of Birth *(month/day/year)*

City	State	Zip Code	Social Security #

I am aware that federal law provides for imprisonment and/or fines for false statements or use of false documents in connection with the completion of this form.

I attest, under penalty of perjury, that I am (check one of the following):

☐ A citizen of the United States

☐ A noncitizen national of the United States (see instructions)

☐ A lawful permanent resident (Alien #)

☐ An alien authorized to work (Alien # or Admission #)
until (expiration date, if applicable - *month/day/year*)

Employee's Signature	Date *(month/day/year)*

Preparer and/or Translator Certification *(To be completed and signed if Section 1 is prepared by a person other than the employee.)* I attest, under penalty of perjury, that I have assisted in the completion of this form and that to the best of my knowledge the information is true and correct.

Preparer's/Translator's Signature	Print Name

Address *(Street Name and Number, City, State, Zip Code)*	Date *(month/day/year)*

Section 2. Employer Review and Verification *(To be completed and signed by employer. Examine one document from List A OR examine one document from List B and one from List C, as listed on the reverse of this form, and record the title, number, and expiration date, if any, of the document(s).)*

List A	OR	List B	AND	List C
Document title:				
Issuing authority:				
Document #:				
Expiration Date *(if any)*:				
Document #:				
Expiration Date *(if any)*:				

CERTIFICATION: I attest, under penalty of perjury, that I have examined the document(s) presented by the above-named employee, that the above-listed document(s) appear to be genuine and to relate to the employee named, that the employee began employment on *(month/day/year)* and that to the best of my knowledge the employee is authorized to work in the United States. (State employment agencies may omit the date the employee began employment.)

Signature of Employer or Authorized Representative	Print Name	Title

Business or Organization Name and Address *(Street Name and Number, City, State, Zip Code)*	Date *(month/day/year)*
IRS-HCO, 5333 Getwell Rd., Memphis, TN, 38116	

Section 3. Updating and Reverification *(To be completed and signed by employer.)*

A. New Name *(if applicable)*	B. Date of Rehire *(month/day/year)* *(if applicable)*

C. If employee's previous grant of work authorization has expired, provide the information below for the document that establishes current employment authorization.

Document Title:	Document #:	Expiration Date *(if any)*:

I attest, under penalty of perjury, that to the best of my knowledge, this employee is authorized to work in the United States, and if the employee presented document(s), the document(s) I have examined appear to be genuine and to relate to the individual.

Signature of Employer or Authorized Representative	Date *(month/day/year)*

IRS Form SS-4 – Application for Employer Identification Number

If you have a business, it is a great idea to have an EIN. This is a nine-digit number that is assigned to sole proprietors, corporations, partnerships, estates, trusts, and other entities that will be used for filing and reporting taxes.

Form **SS-4** (Rev. December 2017) Department of the Treasury Internal Revenue Service	**Application for Employer Identification Number** (For use by employers, corporations, partnerships, trusts, estates, churches, government agencies, Indian tribal entities, certain individuals, and others.) ▶ Go to www.irs.gov/FormSS4 for instructions and the latest information. ▶ See separate instructions for each line. ▶ Keep a copy for your records.	OMB No. 1545-0003 EIN

Type or print clearly.

1 Legal name of entity (or individual) for whom the EIN is being requested

2 Trade name of business (if different from name on line 1)	3 Executor, administrator, trustee, "care of" name
4a Mailing address (room, apt., suite no. and street, or P.O. box)	5a Street address (if different) (Do not enter a P.O. box.)
4b City, state, and ZIP code (if foreign, see instructions)	5b City, state, and ZIP code (if foreign, see instructions)

6 County and state where principal business is located

7a Name of responsible party	7b SSN, ITIN, or EIN

8a Is this application for a limited liability company (LLC) (or a foreign equivalent)? ☐ Yes ☐ No	8b If 8a is "Yes," enter the number of LLC members ▶

8c If 8a is "Yes," was the LLC organized in the United States? . . . . ☐ Yes ☐ No

9a Type of entity (check only one box). Caution. If 8a is "Yes," see the instructions for the correct box to check.
☐ Sole proprietor (SSN)
☐ Partnership
☐ Corporation (enter form number to be filed) ▶
☐ Personal service corporation
☐ Church or church-controlled organization
☐ Other nonprofit organization (specify) ▶
☐ Other (specify) ▶
☐ Estate (SSN of decedent)
☐ Plan administrator (TIN)
☐ Trust (TIN of grantor)
☐ Military/National Guard   ☐ State/local government
☐ Farmers' cooperative   ☐ Federal government
☐ REMIC   ☐ Indian tribal governments/enterprises
Group Exemption Number (GEN) if any ▶

9b If a corporation, name the state or foreign country (if applicable) where incorporated | State | Foreign country |

10 Reason for applying (check only one box)
☐ Started new business (specify type) ▶
☐ Hired employees (Check the box and see line 13.)
☐ Compliance with IRS withholding regulations
☐ Other (specify) ▶
☐ Banking purpose (specify purpose) ▶
☐ Changed type of organization (specify new type) ▶
☐ Purchased going business
☐ Created a trust (specify type) ▶
☐ Created a pension plan (specify type) ▶

11 Date business started or acquired (month, day, year). See instructions.	12 Closing month of accounting year

13 Highest number of employees expected in the next 12 months (enter -0- if none). If no employees expected, skip line 14.	14 If you expect your employment tax liability to be $1,000 or less in a full calendar year and want to file Form 944 annually instead of Forms 941 quarterly, check here. (Your employment tax liability generally will be $1,000 or less if you expect to pay $4,000 or less in total wages.) If you do not check this box, you must file Form 941 for every quarter. ☐
Agricultural	Household	Other	

15 First date wages or annuities were paid (month, day, year). Note: If applicant is a withholding agent, enter date income will first be paid to nonresident alien (month, day, year) . . . . ▶

16 Check one box that best describes the principal activity of your business. ☐ Health care & social assistance ☐ Wholesale-agent/broker
☐ Construction ☐ Rental & leasing ☐ Transportation & warehousing ☐ Accommodation & food service ☐ Wholesale-other ☐ Retail
☐ Real estate ☐ Manufacturing ☐ Finance & insurance ☐ Other (specify) ▶

17 Indicate principal line of merchandise sold, specific construction work done, products produced, or services provided.

18 Has the applicant entity shown on line 1 ever applied for and received an EIN? ☐ Yes ☐ No
If "Yes," write previous EIN here ▶

Third Party Designee	Complete this section only if you want to authorize the named individual to receive the entity's EIN and answer questions about the completion of this form.	
	Designee's name	Designee's telephone number (include area code)
	Address and ZIP code	Designee's fax number (include area code)

Under penalties of perjury, I declare that I have examined this application, and to the best of my knowledge and belief, it is true, correct, and complete. | Applicant's telephone number (include area code)

Name and title (type or print clearly) ▶

| Signature ▶ | Date ▶ | Applicant's fax number (include area code) |

For Privacy Act and Paperwork Reduction Act Notice, see separate instructions.   Cat. No. 16055N   Form **SS-4** (Rev. 12-2017)

IRS Form W-2 – Wage and Tax Statement

By January 31, you are required to report and give each employee a W-2 that reports the totals for wages, federal taxes, state taxes, and any other withholding from their pay throughout the year. This form is highly important to your employees for filing their individual taxes.

22222	a Employee's social security number	OMB No. 1545-0008		
b Employer identification number (EIN)			1 Wages, tips, other compensation	2 Federal income tax withheld
c Employer's name, address, and ZIP code			3 Social security wages	4 Social security tax withheld
			5 Medicare wages and tips	6 Medicare tax withheld
			7 Social security tips	8 Allocated tips
d Control number			9 Verification code	10 Dependent care benefits
e Employee's first name and initial Last name		Suff.	11 Nonqualified plans	12a
			13 Statutory employee Retirement plan Third party sick pay	12b
			14 Other	12c
				12d
f Employee's address and ZIP code				
15 State Employer's state ID number	16 State wages, tips, etc.	17 State income tax	18 Local wages, tips, etc.	19 Local income tax 20 Locality name

Form **W-2** Wage and Tax Statement   **2017**   Department of the Treasury—Internal Revenue Service

Copy 1—For State, City, or Local Tax Department

IRS Form W-3 – Transmittal of Wage and Tax Statements

Form W-3 is transmitted with form W-2s to the Social Security Administration (SSA). It will show the Social Security wages, Medicare wages and the withholdings for all your employees.

DO NOT STAPLE OR FOLD

33333	a Control number	For Official Use Only ▶ OMB No. 1545-0008		

b Kind of Payer (Check one)	941-SS ☐ Military ☐ 943 ☐ 944 ☐ Hshld. emp. ☐ Medicare govt. emp. ☐	Kind of Employer (Check one)	None apply ☐ 501c non-govt. ☐ State/local non 501c ☐ State/local 501c ☐ Federal govt. ☐	Third-party sick pay (Check if applicable) ☐

c Total number of Forms W-2	d Establishment number	1 Wages, tips, other compensation	2 Income tax withheld
e Employer identification number (EIN)		3 Social security wages	4 Social security tax withheld
f Employer's name		5 Medicare wages and tips	6 Medicare tax withheld
		7 Social security tips	8
		9	10
g Employer's address and ZIP code		11 Nonqualified plans	12a Deferred compensation
h Other EIN used this year		13 For third-party sick pay use only	12b
15 Employer's territorial ID number		14 Income tax withheld by payer of third party sick pay	
Employer's contact person		Employer's telephone number	For Official Use Only
Employer's fax number		Employer's email address	

Copy 1—For Local Tax Department

Under penalties of perjury, I declare that I have examined this return and accompanying documents, and, to the best of my knowledge and belief, they are true, correct, and complete.

Signature ▶ _____ Title ▶ _____ Date ▶ _____

Form W-3SS Transmittal of Wage and Tax Statements   2018   Department of the Treasury Internal Revenue Service

Where To File

For more information about where to file Copy 1, contact your state, city, or local tax department.

American Samoa. File Copy 1 of Form W-3SS and Forms W-2AS at the following address.

American Samoa Tax Office
Executive Office Building
First Floor
Pago Pago, AS 96799

Guam. File Copy 1 of Form W-3SS and Forms W-2GU at the following address.

Guam Department of Revenue and Taxation
P.O. Box 23607
GMF, GU 96921

U.S. Virgin Islands. File Copy 1 of Form W-3SS and Forms W-2VI at the following address.

Virgin Islands Bureau of Internal Revenue
6115 Estate Smith Bay
Suite 225
St. Thomas, VI 00802

Commonwealth of the Northern Mariana Islands. File Form OS-3710 and Copy 1 of Forms W-2CM at the following address.

Division of Revenue and Taxation
Commonwealth of the Northern Mariana Islands
P.O. Box 5234 CHRB
Saipan, MP 96950

IRS Form W-4 – Employees Withholding Allowance Certificate

Form W-4 is used to withhold the correct amount of federal income taxes from the employee's paycheck. A recommendation by the IRS is for the employees to submit an updated form each year.

Form W-4 (2017)

Purpose. Complete Form W-4 so that your employer can withhold the correct federal income tax from your pay. Consider completing a new Form W-4 each year and when your personal or financial situation changes.

Exemption from withholding. If you are exempt, complete only lines 1, 2, 3, 4, and 7 and sign the form to validate it. Your exemption for 2017 expires February 15, 2018. See Pub. 505, Tax Withholding and Estimated Tax.

Note: If another person can claim you as a dependent on his or her tax return, you can't claim exemption from withholding if your total income exceeds $1,050 and includes more than $350 of unearned income (for example, interest and dividends).

Exceptions. An employee may be able to claim exemption from withholding even if the employee is a dependent, if the employee:
- Is age 65 or older,
- Is blind, or
- Will claim adjustments to income; tax credits; or itemized deductions, on his or her tax return.

The exceptions don't apply to supplemental wages greater than $1,000,000.

Basic instructions. If you aren't exempt, complete the **Personal Allowances Worksheet** below. The worksheets on page 2 further adjust your withholding allowances based on itemized deductions, certain credits, adjustments to income, or two-earners/multiple jobs situations.

Complete all worksheets that apply. However, you may claim fewer (or zero) allowances. For regular wages, withholding must be based on allowances you claimed and may not be a flat amount or percentage of wages.

Head of household. Generally, you can claim head of household filing status on your tax return only if you are unmarried and pay more than 50% of the costs of keeping up a home for yourself and your dependent(s) or other qualifying individuals. See Pub. 501, Exemptions, Standard Deduction, and Filing Information, for information.

Tax credits. You can take projected tax credits into account in figuring your allowable number of withholding allowances. Credits for child or dependent care expenses and the child tax credit may be claimed using the **Personal Allowances Worksheet** below. See Pub. 505 for information on converting your other credits into withholding allowances.

Nonwage income. If you have a large amount of nonwage income, such as interest or dividends, consider making estimated tax payments using Form 1040-ES, Estimated Tax for Individuals. Otherwise, you may owe additional tax. If you have pension or annuity income, see Pub. 505 to find out if you should adjust your withholding on Form W-4 or W-4P.

Two earners or multiple jobs. If you have a working spouse or more than one job, figure the total number of allowances you are entitled to claim on all jobs using worksheets from only one Form W-4. Your withholding usually will be most accurate when all allowances are claimed on the Form W-4 for the highest paying job and zero allowances are claimed on the others. See Pub. 505 for details.

Nonresident alien. If you are a nonresident alien, see Notice 1392, Supplemental Form W-4 Instructions for Nonresident Aliens, before completing this form.

Check your withholding. After your Form W-4 takes effect, use Pub. 505 to see how the amount you are having withheld compares to your projected total tax for 2017. See Pub. 505, especially if your earnings exceed $130,000 (Single) or $180,000 (Married).

Future developments. Information about any future developments affecting Form W-4 (such as legislation enacted after we release it) will be posted at www.irs.gov/w4.

Personal Allowances Worksheet (Keep for your records.)

A	Enter "1" for **yourself** if no one else can claim you as a dependent	A ___
B	Enter "1" if: { • You're single and have only one job; or • You're married, have only one job, and your spouse doesn't work; or • Your wages from a second job or your spouse's wages (or the total of both) are $1,500 or less. }	B ___
C	Enter "1" for your **spouse**. But, you may choose to enter "-0-" if you are married and have either a working spouse or more than one job. (Entering "-0-" may help you avoid having too little tax withheld.)	C ___
D	Enter number of **dependents** (other than your spouse or yourself) you will claim on your tax return	D ___
E	Enter "1" if you will file as **head of household** on your tax return (see conditions under **Head of household** above)	E ___
F	Enter "1" if you have at least $2,000 of **child or dependent care expenses** for which you plan to claim a credit . . .	F ___
	(Note: Do **not** include child support payments. See Pub. 503, Child and Dependent Care Expenses, for details.)	
G	**Child Tax Credit** (including additional child tax credit). See Pub. 972, Child Tax Credit, for more information. • If your total income will be less than $70,000 ($100,000 if married), enter "2" for each eligible child; then **less** "1" if you have two to four eligible children or **less** "2" if you have five or more eligible children. • If your total income will be between $70,000 and $84,000 ($100,000 and $119,000 if married), enter "1" for each eligible child.	G ___
H	Add lines A through G and enter total here. **(Note:** This may be different from the number of exemptions you claim on your tax return.) ▶	H ___

For accuracy, complete all worksheets that apply.	• If you plan to **itemize or claim adjustments to income** and want to reduce your withholding, see the **Deductions and Adjustments Worksheet** on page 2. • If you are **single and have more than one job** or are **married and you and your spouse both work** and the combined earnings from all jobs exceed $50,000 ($20,000 if married), see the **Two-Earners/Multiple Jobs Worksheet** on page 2 to avoid having too little tax withheld. • If **neither** of the above situations applies, **stop here** and enter the number from line H on line 5 of Form W-4 below.

---------- Separate here and give Form W-4 to your employer. Keep the top part for your records. ----------

Form W-4 — Employee's Withholding Allowance Certificate

Department of the Treasury
Internal Revenue Service

▶ Whether you are entitled to claim a certain number of allowances or exemption from withholding is subject to review by the IRS. Your employer may be required to send a copy of this form to the IRS.

OMB No. 1545-0074

2017

1 Your first name and middle initial	Last name		2 Your social security number

Home address (number and street or rural route)	3 ☐ Single ☐ Married ☐ Married, but withhold at higher Single rate.
City or town, state, and ZIP code	**Note:** If married, but legally separated, or spouse is a nonresident alien, check the "Single" box. 4 If your last name differs from that shown on your social security card, check here. You must call 1-800-772-1213 for a replacement card. ▶ ☐

5	Total number of allowances you are claiming (from line H above or from the applicable worksheet on page 2)	5 ___
6	Additional amount, if any, you want withheld from each paycheck	6 $ ___
7	I claim exemption from withholding for 2017, and I certify that I meet **both** of the following conditions for exemption. • Last year I had a right to a refund of **all** federal income tax withheld because I had **no** tax liability, **and** • This year I expect a refund of **all** federal income tax withheld because I expect to have **no** tax liability. If you meet both conditions, write "Exempt" here . . . . ▶	7 ___

Under penalties of perjury, I declare that I have examined this certificate and, to the best of my knowledge and belief, it is true, correct, and complete.

Employee's signature
(This form is not valid unless you sign it.) ▶   Date ▶

8 Employer's name and address (Employer: Complete lines 8 and 10 only if sending to the IRS.)	9 Office code (optional)	10 Employer identification number (EIN)

For Privacy Act and Paperwork Reduction Act Notice, see page 2.   Cat. No. 10220Q   Form **W-4** (2017)

Deductions and Adjustments Worksheet

Note: Use this worksheet only if you plan to itemize deductions or claim certain credits or adjustments to income.

1 Enter an estimate of your 2017 itemized deductions. These include qualifying home mortgage interest, charitable contributions, state and local taxes, medical expenses in excess of 10% of your income, and miscellaneous deductions. For 2017, you may have to reduce your itemized deductions if your income is over $313,800 and you're married filing jointly or you're a qualifying widow(er); $287,650 if you're head of household; $261,500 if you're single, not head of household and not a qualifying widow(er); or $156,900 if you're married filing separately. See Pub. 505 for details . . . . **1** $ ____

2 Enter: { $12,700 if married filing jointly or qualifying widow(er) }
$9,350 if head of household
$6,350 if single or married filing separately . . . . **2** $ ____

3 Subtract line 2 from line 1. If zero or less, enter "-0-" . . . . **3** $ ____

4 Enter an estimate of your 2017 adjustments to income and any additional standard deduction (see Pub. 505) **4** $ ____

5 **Add** lines 3 and 4 and enter the total. (Include any amount for credits from the *Converting Credits to Withholding Allowances for 2017 Form W-4* worksheet in Pub. 505.) . . . . **5** $ ____

6 Enter an estimate of your 2017 nonwage income (such as dividends or interest) . . . . **6** $ ____

7 **Subtract** line 6 from line 5. If zero or less, enter "-0-" . . . . **7** $ ____

8 **Divide** the amount on line 7 by $4,050 and enter the result here. Drop any fraction . . . . . . **8** ____

9 Enter the number from the **Personal Allowances Worksheet**, line H, page 1 . . . . **9** ____

10 **Add** lines 8 and 9 and enter the total here. If you plan to use the **Two-Earners/Multiple Jobs Worksheet**, also enter this total on line 1 below. Otherwise, **stop here** and enter this total on Form W-4, line 5, page 1 **10** ____

Two-Earners/Multiple Jobs Worksheet (See *Two earners or multiple jobs* on page 1.)

Note: Use this worksheet only if the instructions under line H on page 1 direct you here.

1 Enter the number from line H, page 1 (or from line 10 above if you used the **Deductions and Adjustments Worksheet**) **1** ____

2 Find the number in **Table 1** below that applies to the **LOWEST** paying job and enter it here. **However,** if you are married filing jointly and wages from the highest paying job are $65,000 or less, do not enter more than "3" . . . . **2** ____

3 If line 1 is **more than or equal to** line 2, subtract line 2 from line 1. Enter the result here (if zero, enter "-0-") and on Form W-4, line 5, page 1. **Do not** use the rest of this worksheet . . . . **3** ____

Note: If line 1 is **less than** line 2, enter "-0-" on Form W-4, line 5, page 1. Complete lines 4 through 9 below to figure the additional withholding amount necessary to avoid a year-end tax bill.

4 Enter the number from line 2 of this worksheet . . . . **4** ____

5 Enter the number from line 1 of this worksheet . . . . **5** ____

6 **Subtract** line 5 from line 4 . . . . **6** ____

7 Find the amount in **Table 2** below that applies to the **HIGHEST** paying job and enter it here . . . . **7** $ ____

8 **Multiply** line 7 by line 6 and enter the result here. This is the additional annual withholding needed . . **8** $ ____

9 Divide line 8 by the number of pay periods remaining in 2017. For example, divide by 25 if you are paid every two weeks and you complete this form on a date in January when there are 25 pay periods remaining in 2017. Enter the result here and on Form W-4, line 6, page 1. This is the additional amount to be withheld from each paycheck **9** $ ____

Table 1				Table 2			
Married Filing Jointly		**All Others**		**Married Filing Jointly**		**All Others**	
If wages from LOWEST paying job are—	Enter on line 2 above	If wages from LOWEST paying job are—	Enter on line 2 above	If wages from HIGHEST paying job are—	Enter on line 7 above	If wages from HIGHEST paying job are—	Enter on line 7 above
$0 - $7,000	0	$0 - $8,000	0	$0 - $75,000	$610	$0 - $38,000	$610
7,001 - 14,000	1	8,001 - 16,000	1	75,001 - 135,000	1,010	38,001 - 85,000	1,010
14,001 - 22,000	2	16,001 - 26,000	2	135,001 - 205,000	1,130	85,001 - 185,000	1,130
22,001 - 27,000	3	26,001 - 34,000	3	205,001 - 360,000	1,340	185,001 - 400,000	1,340
27,001 - 35,000	4	34,001 - 44,000	4	360,001 - 405,000	1,420	400,001 and over	1,600
35,001 - 44,000	5	44,001 - 70,000	5	405,001 and over	1,600		
44,001 - 55,000	6	70,001 - 85,000	6				
55,001 - 65,000	7	85,001 - 110,000	7				
65,001 - 75,000	8	110,001 - 125,000	8				
75,001 - 80,000	9	125,001 - 140,000	9				
80,001 - 95,000	10	140,001 and over	10				
95,001 - 115,000	11						
115,001 - 130,000	12						
130,001 - 140,000	13						
140,001 - 150,000	14						
150,001 and over	15						

Conclusion

I know this is a lot of information to take in. It does not matter if you are in a partnership, self-employed or a limited liability company, taxes are a way of life. Each year, as a business owner, you will be faced with the challenges of confronting the IRS and taking them by the horns as you attempt to file your business and individual taxes.

This time of year seems to scare taxpayers. Sometimes you do not know where to begin. If you follow the simple guidance throughout these chapters, preparing and keeping track of your taxable income and expenses throughout the year will be easy. This will make tax time easier as you will have all the proper documents needed for your taxes.

Even if you use a tax specialist, it is highly important to know and understand what you can deduct and what credits are available to you. Be aware of what is available to you and do your research.

President Trump signed a new tax bill in December 2017. These new figures have been included here. However, there is so much in this new bill that it would be a great idea to learn what is in it. Do not rely on your tax specialist knowing the ins and outs. Yes, they do know, although through the proper research you can ask the right questions to ensure you receive the maximum return on your money.

As a special bonus I included many forms you will be using in your small business. Even though a tax specialist will help you with this, it is always a great idea to have them read so they can review them.

"Knowledge is power!" That is the motto I live by. Check out the IRS website as they give you all the answers to an open book test. Now that you have been given the knowledge and awareness, the action is up to you.

Use this book as a guide to remind you of what needs to be accomplished in your business to prepare for your taxes. Do not make it a task you do at the last minute when it is time to file your taxes. Start preparing for the next tax season in January. It is a task that should be looked at every month throughout the entire year so you can get the most out of your business.

Do not let the IRS scare you. With the tools you have been given, those audits and communications from the IRS will seem like a small thing. A great motto is, "be prepared!" Keep accurate records and do not try to hide anything from the IRS and you are golden. Preparation and alertness is the key.

Start making IRS work for you and your business. Capitalize on what they have to offer. Keep good records. Know your deductions. Know the credits offered to you and add value to your business by getting a great return.

Best of luck with all your endeavours. I look forward to hearing about the great success you will be having.

Greg Shields

Preview of Bookkeeping

The Ultimate Guide to Bookkeeping for Small Business

Introduction

Whether you are just starting your business or have had your business for years, it is important to know bookkeeping.

Bookkeeping has been around for centuries. However, it has evolved over time to better help your business keep track of your finances.

Bookkeeping covers a long list of aspects that help the business owner make decisions about the company. To better understand bookkeeping, my goal is to help you get a good feel for knowing how to read the financial reports, the basics of bookkeeping, employees, understanding the balance sheet and income statement, and so much more.

Come along with me as we explore the world of bookkeeping and help you, the business owner, understand how to make sense out of bookkeeping.

As an added bonus, I have included a section for your business taxes. I also included a step-by-step process of preparing W-2 forms and the information that is needed for those. You will soon find out that there is more to it than just providing the information and typing it up on the W-2 form.

Keep reading and you will see what it takes to get on the same page as your bookkeeper. I always said, "It is not the business owner that runs the business. It is the business owner teamed up with the bookkeeper that truly runs the business."

Running a business can be fun and rewarding. However, if you do not have the basic knowledge of the fundamental financial skills needed, it can prove to be stressful as well.

Throughout this book you will learn the basics of bookkeeping and finding the right bookkeeper for you. As you go through it, you will also learn about the ledgers and journals. It is important that you know where your money is at all times. I also take the time to talk to you about hiring employees. Let's face it, if your business is going to grow above a certain level, you will eventually need to hire someone to work with you.

There is also a lot of software available to help you with all your bookkeeping needs, although not all accounting software is right for your business. We will take a look at a few of the top rated applications and give you both the good and bad of each one.

Don't forget, you also need to understand those scary financial statements. That's why we will take a look at the four main financial statements and break them down for you so that you can easily read and understand each one.

It does not matter if you have been in business for a couple of years or are just starting, you will be filing taxes at the end of the year. This is a lot of work and your bookkeeper can help you get prepared. Within the bonus chapter, I included a checklist for small businesses to help you along the way in knowing which documents you need to find and hold on to.

Did you know that as a business owner you can deduct a lot of your expenses? I included that as well. It is only a small list, and with a little research you could probably find more.

Finally, I also included, in detail, how to go about preparing, distributing, and filing the employees' W-2's.

So come along with me as we take this glorious adventure into bookkeeping for small businesses and give you the power to understand your businesses financial health.

Chapter 1 – Bookkeeping Basics

Before we get started on breaking down bookkeeping, we need to look at some of the basics. I want you to have the ability to read your financial records and understand them. This will allow for you to know the financial aspect of your business. In turn, it will allow you to make good decisions that can increase the growth of your business.

Double-Entry Method

Bookkeeping uses a method called the "Double-Entry Bookkeeping." This means that for every entry there is at least one debit and one credit.

I want you to remember this equation:

- Assets = Liabilities + Equity

This is the basic formula for the Double-Entry Method and will come into play with every transaction you make.

Source Documents

Every transaction made will have a source document. Source documents could be anything from a contract to a gas receipt. If you spent the business's money then you will need some form of proof of how much you spent. These are the source documents.

These documents will give us all the information you will need to record it in the books. This includes referencing the source documents. Some software will allow you to attach the scanned file to the transaction so that at any time you can bring up the source document.

End-Of-Period Procedures

End-of-Period Procedures relate to not only quarters. Even though all the transactions have been recorded throughout the months or year, they still are not read for preparing the financial reports.

To ensure that you have your books accurate for preparing the financial reports, you need to consider that there are procedures that need to happen at least at month-end, year-end, and the end of payroll year.

The following outline will show, as a guideline, what should be done during each time.

1. Month-End Procedures
   o Run the Company/Business Data Auditor
   o Reconcile your Bank Accounts
   o Review Reports
   o Send Customer Statements
   o Record Depreciation
   o Pay Payroll Taxes
   o Lock Periods

2. Year-End Procedures (to prepare for the new fiscal year)
   o Complete Month-End Tasks
   o Perform an Inventory Count
   o Provide Information to your Accountant
   o Enter End-of-Year Adjustments
   o Back Up your Company/Business File
   o Start New Fiscal Year
   o Optimize and Verify your Company/Business File

3. End of Payroll Year (to prepare for new fiscal year) - *NOTE: Do Not Update Tax Tables*

   o Run Your Last Payroll

   o Optimize and Verify your Company/Business File

   o Back Up your Company/Business File

   o Start a New Payroll Year

   o Install Product Updates

   o Run Your First Payroll

   o Restore Your Backup

   o Print Year-End Payroll Forms

   o Print Vendor 1099 Statements

   o Print Payroll Reports

Compile the Adjusted Trial Balance

Making these adjustments are very important. When looking at which adjustments need to be made first, you need to gather and compile a spreadsheet that will allow for your trial balance entries as well as the adjustments.

Keep in mind that these adjustments are for correcting errors in the initial trial balance so that everything will come to balance. This form for the adjustments is an internal form but will be used for helping compile the financial statements. Now that automated systems like Xero and QuickBooks are used, the trial balance worksheet is not often practiced. However, it is still a good source document. This is in part due to the automated systems creating the reports for you.

Here is an example of what the worksheet may look like:

Frank's Financials

Trial Balance

August 31, 20XX

	Unadjusted Trial Balance	Adjusted Entries	Adjusted Trial Balance
Cash	$60,000		$60,000
Accounts Receivable	$180,000	$50,000	$230,000
Inventory	$300,000		$300,000
Fixed Assets (net)	$210,000		$210,000
Accounts Payable	($90,000)		($90,000)
Accrued Liabilities	($50,000)	($25,000)	($75,000)
Notes Payable	($420,000)		($420,000)
Equity	($350,000)		($350,000)
Revenue	($400,000)	($50,000)	($450,000)
Cost of Goods Sold	$290,000		$290,000
Salaries	$200,000	$25,000	$225,000
Payroll Taxes	$20,000		$20,000
Rent	$35,000		$35,000
Other Expenses	$15,000		$15,000
Totals	$0.00	$0.00	$0.00

Closing the Books

When closing your books at the end of a fiscal year, there are 4 areas that will need to be closed. These areas are temporary accounts and should be zeroed out at the end of each fiscal year.

First, create an Income Summary account. This is considered a holding area.

Closing the Revenue Accounts

The first area that needs to be addressed are the revenue accounts. You will either Debit or Credit this account to close it out and have a zero balance. Then you will either Debit or Credit the Income Summary account to add that balance to the account. Remember if you Debit or Credit one account you must do the opposite for the other account to keep the books balanced.

Closing the Expense Accounts

The second set of accounts are the expense accounts. You will do the same with these accounts as you did with the Revenue accounts. You must close out all expense accounts.

Balancing the Income Summary

By name you should have an increase in the income summary for the revenue and a decrease for each of the expenses. Keep in mind that if the expenses are more than the revenue then it will be a negative number and considered a loss. However, if the revenue is more than the expenses then it is a gain or profit for that year.

Closing the Income Summary

The last step in closing the book is to Debit or Credit the income summary account and do the same to the Retained Earnings Account, leaving a zero balance in the income summary account.

Preparing Reports

A pretty important step is to prepare the reports or financial statements. Although there are so many reports that can be created, we are going to focus on the main reports as they are what is needed for a small business.

As a bookkeeper, you will need to get very familiar with the following reports:

- The Balance Sheet
- Income Statement
- Statement of Retained Earnings
- Statement of Cash Flow

Later in this book we will look more closely at each one of these statements and how to read them so that you can make sense out of your businesses financial standings.

Check out this book!

Preview of Accounting

The Ultimate Guide to Accounting for Beginners – Learn the Basic Accounting Principles

Introduction

This book is intended for people who want to know something about the fundamentals of financial accounting without becoming an accountant. Many people are in this position; small business owners, employers, employees, business owners, stockholders, investors, and many, many more. Most of these folks do not need a deep understanding of accounting, they just need to learn what accounting is and how they should be using it. Just as important, they need to understand what accountants are talking about in their reports. They must learn the vocabulary and the most important terms. The product of accounting is information, important information for that wide range of stakeholders.

We will examine this subject in some detail, discussing accounting fundamentals, the various areas where accounting professionals work and the information they produce. We will also examine the measures and ratios that accountants use to analyze an organization's performance and the important relationship between time and money. The fact that information is the product of accounting will remain foremost in this book.

Chapter 1 - Accounting is Different From Bookkeeping

Accounting is not bookkeeping. Bookkeeping concentrates on recording the organization's financial activities, whatever the business in which they are engaged. Maybe that is retail sales, home construction or manufacturing. No matter what business activity is taking place, someone must keep track of the transactions; selling, buying, repairing equipment, everything of significance. And in fact, even individuals must learn about accounting and must do certain bookkeeping tasks for their own personal finances, like balancing their checkbook and establishing personal budgets.

If the business is engaged in retail sales, bookkeepers record every sale, every purchase of inventory and every employee's pay. That is bookkeeping.

Accountants take this information and analyze, summarize and report the results. Remember, the product of accounting is information. This information is vital to management for their operating and investment decisions. Management must know how much money the business has, how much inventory it holds, how many employees are retained and how much they are being paid.

The viewpoint of a bookkeeper is the details. The viewpoint of an accountant is much broader and at a higher level. The accountant must be able to advise management on many decisions; how many more employees can be hired, what taxes are due and how to minimize them, analyzing investment decisions, and so forth.

Let's look at an example. Riverside Machine Company is a small manufacturer of components for the automobile industry. Their clients include almost all of the automobile manufacturers, and they are very busy when the industry is thriving.

The owners of Riverside are concerned about reducing manufacturing costs for a certain type of part that requires a lot of machining on several different types of machines. The engineers have determined that they can increase the rate of production by installing robots to load and unload the machines and transfer parts between them. The company has several robotic systems in operation now and is confident of their ability to incorporate these new robots. Currently, there is a serious backlog of work for these machines and improving the workflow would allow faster delivery with less overtime and not needing to work weekends to maintain production.

The engineers have determined all the necessary information related to this investment in terms of robot costs, tools needed by the robots, increases in production rate and effect on delivery time. They then sit down with the accounting experts to compute the improvements in cost, reductions in labor costs, shortening of delivery time and so forth. The accountant then uses all of this information to compute the effects on the firm's financial performance and profitability.

In most companies, the accountants compute a value for "Internal Rate of Return" for decisions by management. This rate of return serves as a threshold for new projects. It becomes one of the considerations used by management to decide whether or not to make the investment, in this case, in the new robots. Other considerations of course include delivery improvements, customer satisfaction, product quality and several others. That is a proper role for the accountant working with the engineers.

In addition to being a source of reliable financial information on these kinds of decisions, the accounting department also acts as what can be described as a "Scorekeeper", by monitoring costs and revenues, leading to profitability for the firm. This information is reported to management on a regular basis to help guide ongoing management decisions. The accountants cannot do much at all to influence the profitability of the firm directly, but their role is to report findings to management for them to make decisions.

The accounting function also leads the efforts at budgeting and budget reporting. These are more examples of the accounting product of information. These reports are available in varying levels of detail for publically owned companies and non-profit organizations. Privately owned companies are not required to publish these reports, except for those required by the government, regulatory and taxing authorities.

In their role as providers of information, they are often called upon for informed recommendations to help management decision making.

Chapter 2 - Understanding the Vocabulary

Every special area of interest has its own vocabulary, and accounting is the same. Many of the words used will be familiar to the reader but may have certain shades of meaning that are important. We need to understand this vocabulary. Here are some key definitions that are important to the accounting function.

Asset: an asset is anything the organization owns that helps it accomplish its mission. For a fast food restaurant, the grill or stove in the kitchen area is an asset. For a retail store, the inventory in the back room is an asset, along with display cases and shelves.

Liability: a liability is anything the organization owes to someone else. Unpaid wages to employees is a liability, taxes owed to the local government is a liability, unpaid insurance premiums for employee healthcare policies is a liability, bills for inventory that have not been paid is a liability.

Equity: equity is a measure of the claim of someone on the assets of the organization, such as liabilities (claims by the person or entity to whom the liability is owed, such as loans from a bank) and the investment by the owners of the organization.

Income: money flowing into the organization from its operations in whatever the line of business might be, for example, sales in a fast food restaurant, or rent collected on property the business owns.

Expense: this is the amount of money the organization needs to spend in order to carry out its operations. This represents payments to asset and service providers. For example, payments to a supplier of inventory items for a retail store.

Distributions: outflows of money to owners or stockholders, or bonuses to employees at the end of the year, for example.

Cash Flow: the term cash flow represents the money flowing through the operation, essentially income minus expenses. You can imagine a stream of money flowing into the organization with small streams going out as distributaries to pay for liabilities. The flow that is moving through this stream is the cash flow. How much is left at the end of the process is the profit for the firm.

Overhead: this is a group of costs not directly associated with the major function of the organization but necessary in order to make the organization accomplish its goals. For example, in a hospital, the janitorial staff that cleans and sanitizes the buildings, rooms and equipment are not directly associated with the hospital's patients, but they are absolutely essential. The labor and other costs like cleaning and sanitizing supplies are part of the organization's overhead. All the other myriad of costs like electricity, lighting, lawn maintenance, and even sweeping the parking lot are essential but not directly tied to the patients and their care. The accounting office is considered overhead for any organization not involved in the Public Accounting business.

GAAP: This is the term used to describe the Generally Accepted Accounting Principles. This is a set of 'rules' for the accounting profession, which must be followed to assure an accurate description of the financial activities of the organization. GAAP applies to all organizations that function in commerce, public service, and all other sectors of the general economy. Following these GAAP rules assures the public, the stockholders, the donors to non-profit organizations, the owners, employees and the taxing and regulatory authorities that the accounting for the organization is done in accordance with the proper methods and systems.

Each country establishes its own accounting standards but there exists an International Accounting Standards Board responsible for establishing and accrediting accounting standards for all nations who subscribe. Similarly, many countries establish similar Boards, to promulgate and enforce standards through certification and audit systems. These are in the form of standards, conventions and rules. Companies are not necessarily required to follow them but any publicly traded company must conform to the established Accounting Practices.

Chapter 3 – Accounting Reports: The Income Statement

Remember that the product of accounting is information. The three most common forms for that information are the "Income Statement", the "Balance Sheet", and the "Cash Flow Statement." Every organization uses some form of these three documents and usually all three. We will explore the Balance Sheet in Chapter 4 and the Cash Flow Statement in Chapter 5.

The Income Statement or Profit and Loss Statement (or P&L statement) can be imagined as a video tape of the organization over some period of time, like a month, six months or a year. This statement tells management how the firm is doing from the standpoint of "Are we making money or not?" Of course, this is a very fundamental question, since after a number of periods of losses, the firm will no longer be viable and will go out of business.

The most important use of the Income Statement is to compare it with prior periods and with the period budget. If management has determined that the firm must meet certain performance levels, they need the answer to the question above; "How are we doing compared with our goals and budget?" Each organization has an established and agreed upon budget. The budget contains allocations of resources for all of the activities of the organization, from sales, purchases of materials for sale or production, employee salaries and benefits and even overhead items like electricity and water.

These budgets are set up, usually each year, to guide the managers and supervisors in what decisions can be made to commit resources like money and labour, and for what purposes. Based on this budget, which has been agreed upon by management, it acts as a steering mechanism for the firm's operations. The periodic P&L reports represent the Accounting function's role in keeping score. Here is an example of a P&L Statement or an Income Statement. We will look at each of these entries to see what they represent, based on The Martin Company.

THE MARTIN COMPANY, INC.

INCOME STATEMENT

(FIRST HALF, 2014)

JANUARY 1, 2014 THROUGH JUNE 30, 2014

(all amounts in thousands of dollars)

Sales, Gross: $116,410

Less: Returns and Allowances: $3,075

Net Sales: $113,335

Less Cost of Goods Sold: $78,683

Less Current Depreciation Charges: $1,450

Gross Profit: $33,202

Operating Expenses

Selling and Promotion: $18,005

General and Administration: $8,910

Total Operating Expenses: $26,915

Operating Profit: $6,287

(Gross Profit minus Operating Expense)

Other Income and Expense

Interest and Dividend Income: $363

less: Interest Expense: $917

Net Interest Expense: $554

Profit Before Taxes: $5,733

Taxes on Income at 35%: $2,007

Net Profit: $3,726

This P&L or Income Statement is for the Martin Company. The Martin Company manufacturers small household appliances, which are sold through distributors under Martin's label and major discount and department stores under their labels. Manufacturing operations are located in a small town in the Midwest. The key technologies employed by the firm include manufacturing of fractional horsepower motors, injection molding of plastic parts and machining of miscellaneous small metal parts such as shafts, armatures and gears as well as assembly of the products, packaging and shipping them to customers.

As it says at the top, this report covers the first half of the year. For this company, their budget year is a calendar year. Some organizations may use other budget years. Government organizations often use October 1 through September 30 as a budget year. A mid-year report is very valuable to management, to keep track of performance, especially in complex organizations.

Total Sales; The first line entered is the total sales for that period. This is the value of products shipped to customers. In some cases, there may be returns from customers for any number of reasons; wrong color, wrong address, quality issues, and so forth. This is recorded as Returns and Allowances and is subtracted from Gross Sales resulting in Net Sales.

Cost of Goods Sold; The line labeled Cost of Goods Sold represents the cost that Martin incurred in producing the products shipped during that period. That will include the materials and components purchased, the labor used to produce these products and may include machine time if that is the procedure for Martin Company.

Depreciation; Martin Company must also account for the wear and tear on their productive assets ranging from big, expensive plastic injection molding machines to company vehicles. This is a real cost that must be accounted for but is not a cash expense. It is determined by the accounting office and along with the Cost of Goods Sold, reduces the net sales to give the amount of Gross Profit. This loss of value of assets is called depreciation and is subtracted from sales, even though it is not a cash expense. Depreciation will be covered in a later section.

Operating Expenses; However, this is not the complete picture of costs incurred. The items labeled Operating Expenses include the salaries of the supervisors, managers, sales representatives, shipping operators, energy costs like electric power and gas, office expenses for papers, copiers, and the myriad of other costs necessary to produce the products that generate sales income. In some companies, this lump of costs may be referred to as "Overhead." Overhead is a necessary expense and must be included in the budget and in P&L statement. Managers and supervisors work hard to keep Overhead costs to a minimum. Overhead also includes taxes paid on the real estate and other ad valorum taxes. These amounts are shown as Selling and Promotion as well as General and Administrative or G&A. G&A usually includes the Overhead costs.

Operating Profit; After accounting for the Operating Expenses, we are left with the Operating Profit. Operating Profit is the first measure of how effective Martin Company is in carrying out its main objective, making and selling products. Operating Profit is the Gross Profit minus the Operating Expenses.

Other Income and Expense; But, Martin Company must also take into account the other costs such as interest on loans they need to purchase equipment and materials. They may have other incidental income from sources like investments, rental property receipts and royalties. These are all included in the P&L statement but are not part of the major business, making and selling products.

Profit Before Taxes; When all of that is included, we see the Profit Before Taxes or PBT. That profit must be reduced by the taxes paid on the sales and other income, and we finally get to see the profits resulting from the major business of Martin. This is what managers call the "Bottom Line."

Managers and supervisors are vitally concerned with how the P&L Statement compares with the budget and how it is changing over time. Are we earning more profit this year than we did in the same period last year and in prior years? Continual growth in profit makes it possible of Martin to stay in business, producing products, serving customers and employing people. It is also essential to being able to expand the business, adding more products and investing in advanced technologies that customers demand.

ACCOUNTING

THE ULTIMATE GUIDE TO ACCOUNTING FOR BEGINNERS

Learn Basic Accounting Principles

GREG SHIELDS

Check out this book!

Made in the USA
Middletown, DE
01 March 2019